IT IS NO DREAM

BIBLE PROPHECY: FACT OR FANATICISM?

IT IS NO DREAM
BIBLE PROPHECY: FACT OR FANATICISM?

by
Elwood McQuaid

The Friends of Israel Gospel Ministry, Inc.
P.O. Box 908, Bellmawr, NJ 08031

IT IS NO DREAM
BIBLE PROPHECY: FACT OR FANATICISM?

Copyright © 1978
The Friends of Israel Gospel Ministry, Inc.
Bellmawr, NJ 08031

Seventh Edition 1989

Cover by Barbara Alber

Printed in the United States of America
Library of Congress Catalog Card Number 78-51766
ISBN 0-915540-21-5

Dedication

TO THE JEWISH PEOPLE

Particularly to those participants in the successive waves
of Aliyah (Ascenders) returning to Israel from
among the nations.

Acknowledgements

The author acknowledges, with sincere gratitude, the assistance of those whose contributions aided immeasurably in the preparation of this book.

Advisor on Church Relations, Consulate of Israel, New York, for arrangements in Israel.

The Embassy of Israel, Washington, D.C., for photographs and technical advice.

Israel Defense Forces, Tel Aviv, Israel, manuscript review and technical advice.

The World Zionist Agency, Jerusalem, Israel:
> Central Archives, for photographs and materials,
> External Affairs, for interview arrangements and materials,
> Information Centre, for books and materials,
> Immigration and Absorption, for interviews and arrangements.

Rev. Marvin J. Rosenthal, The Friends of Israel Gospel Ministry, Inc., for manuscript review and assistance.

Mrs. Doris B. MacIntyre, for manuscript preparation.

Scores of individuals in Israel and the United States who provided information, encouragement, and advice.

Above all, to my beloved wife Maxine and our children, Jason and Missy, who cheerfully bore the separations and lonely hours while this book was in the making.

Table of Contents

Foreward

From between the paws of the rock-hewn sphinx of Egypt, God brought forth the children of Israel and forged them into a great nation.

Four thousand years have extended their span between Israel's birth, demise, and rebirth as a modern state in May of 1948. This prophesied rebirth is unparalleled in all the annuls of recorded history. No other people, expelled for such a long time, over so wide an area, with so many obstacles, have ever returned to their land as a recognizable and viable entity. Nations more numerous, like flaming meteors, shot across the sky to be remembered no more. The proud Assyrians, the powerful Babylonians, the inflexible Medes and Persians, and other nations too numerous to mention are gone. But the Jew, refusing to be either annihilated or assimilated, remains.

Israel's modern rebirth is clearly not the result of any material dimensions which belong to her. There is nothing global or massive about the state of Israel in political terms. Its territory and independence are considerable in history — but pathetically meager in geography. Her land, excluding occupied areas acquired in the Six-Day War, is about the size of the state of New Jersey. Her population equals that of Philadelphia, the fourth largest city in the United States.

In the calculations of the nuclear century, Israel is an insignificant piece of real estate. Her bridge is fragile; her highway narrow.

Clearly, then, if modern Israel is to be regarded as an incident of universal scope, and she must — if she has any elements of greatness, and she does — then these qualities must be vindicated in the spiritual realm. The existence of the modern state of Israel is an inexplicable enigma, apart from the promises and power of an unchanging and all-powerful God. Israel, plainly and simply, exists because God decreed she should.

1

When, on May 14, 1948, Ben Gurion, Israel's first Prime Minister, declared Israel a free and independent state, her total Jewish population numbered 640,000 souls. In 30 years she absorbed an additional 2,400,000 people from all over the world and from every station of life. She has caused the desert to "blossom like a rose"; developed a technologically advanced nation; and simultaneously fought and won four wars for survival, although dramatically outgunned and outnumbered. Her preservation, no less than her rebirth, has been miraculous.

Peace, nonetheless, continues to be Israel's unrealized goal. And true peace is not simply the cessation of hostilities, but a positive relationship based on justice, equity, and mutual respect. Such a peace cannot be merely national and horizontal — it must first be personal and vertical. In the ultimate sense, there can be no national peace between men until there is personal peace with God. When this peace becomes a reality, the hopes, the dreams, the longings of men of good will will come to fruition through the One who is Israel's Messiah and the world's Deliverer.

Elwood McQuaid, in writing *It Is No Dream*, has rendered a great service to seekers of truth. In an age when men are being magnetically drawn to sensationalism, it is refreshing to read a book that is biblically sane and fluidly written.

The author has repeatedly visited Israel, both before and during the writing, and has included true stores that add a fascinating dimension to *It Is No Dream*.

Israel's past history, present reality, and prophetic destiny touch all peoples and are lofty themes concerning which the inspired authors of the Holy Scriptures had much to say. At no time in the past 3,500 years were their prophetic utterances more contemporary than at this present hour.

Marv Rosenthal

THE JEW

We well recall the wandering Jew
    Bowed low and slow of gait,
Who crept the ghettos, wore the patch,
    Absorbed the scorn and hate.

He sold us matches, bought our rags,
    Sewed clothes, and fixed the shoes.
But seldom would we fraternize,
    Strange ones, we thought, those Jews.

It seemed he never quite belonged,
    His gaze was fixed afar.
It was as though he searched the skies
    To find some rising star.

One day he left, quite suddenly,
    That earnest son of Shem.
"I'm going home; I've found my star:
    Beloved Jerusalem!"

He's down on Ben Yehuda Street,
    Erect and bronzed and trim.
Now we stand by in silent awe
    To hear and learn from him.

E. McQ.

Introduction

My intention in approaching this work was not simply to produce one more volume on Bible prophecy. There are numerous works available which deal effectively with prophetic and dispensational themes. Furthermore, one shrinks from the thought of contributing more sensationalized pages on a subject which all too often make extravagant claims but in actuality deliver little substance.

What I feel can be helpful is a book which scans the entire biblical prophetic program for Israel, and at the same time integrates documented historical insights into the outworking of the divine program for the Jewish people. Essential to this aim is an understanding of the Chosen People, what they have experienced, why they have been thus dealt with, and where their journey through history will finally bring them. I have, therefore, restricted research to predominantly Jewish sources.

Many hours have been spent in Israel researching materials and interviewing individuals in positions which allow them to provide vivid perspectives for the reader. Although specific acknowledgments will be given elsewhere, I must immediately recognize the graciousness, availability, and patience of Israelis who have unhesitatingly cooperated in this venture. Military officials, Zionist Agency personnel, government leaders, and religious representatives have deprived themselves of valuable official and personal time to open offices, libraries, and homes to assist in the compilation and review of projected content. In the United States, responses to my requests were forthcoming in kind from members of the Embassy of Israel staff in Washington and the Jewish Consulate in New York. My earnest and enduring gratitude is offered to these men and women, many of whom have become warm friends, for their assistance.

This book is written from an evangelical Christian point of view. Certainly there are great differences of opinion in the religious views of the author and a majority of those mentioned above. While this is true, and it is understood that official and personal cooperation by Jewish people does not imply an endorsement of Christian content, it is everywhere obvious that the people of Israel wish all segments of our fragmented world to understand the inherent right and desire of the Jewish people to live in peace in the land given to Abraham and his posterity.

My ultimate purpose is twofold:

The first is to assist Christians in their understanding of the Jewish people, their problems, aspirations, and divinely destined place in history; to show, through the unfolding of the prophetic program, the unchallengeable miracle of Israel, her sons, and daughters; to give believers a fresh sense of kinship with the land and the Jewish people, and, consequently, a renewed awareness of the responsibility to share what a sovereign Messiah has accomplished in the lives of true Christians.

The second objective is to help Jewish readers differentiate between a "Christianity" which has heaped scorn, ridicule, and persecution upon a suffering people and true Christians who emulate the genuine spirit of Christ toward the Chosen People of God; to aid Jewish people in their comprehension of the enormous dimensions of their unique relationship to the God of the universe; and to show the faithfulness of Jehovah in delivering all the irrevocable promises to Abraham and his seed.

It is my fervent hope that this book will, in some measure, accomplish these twin purposes. Of course, my readers must judge the relative success of the effort. If I have failed, be assured that the deficiency is in literary skills, not a lack of heart concern for the Jewish people or His Land.

Elwood McQuaid

Who against hope believed in hope, that he might become the father of many nations, according to that which was spoken. So shall thy seed be. He staggered not at the promise of God through unbelief, but was strong in faith, giving glory to God. And being fully persuaded that, what he had promised, he was able also to perform.

Romans 4:18, 20-21

CHAPTER ONE

THE PROPHETIC NATION

A SOLITARY FIGURE watched the sun creep over the lush meadows of his new land. As the light came on, his eyes swept the horizon. To the west, the azure Mediterranean sent rhythmic breakers to wash its coastal sands. Before him lay a breathtaking panorama of plunging descents, rolling plains, and great valleys. Away to the east, the Galilee sparkled against the basalt cliffs of the Golan. Clearly visible was the point where the Jordan quit the southern tip of Kinneret to furrow a serpentine course through the land and eventually found its terminus beneath the vaporous haze marking the place where the Dead Sea patiently garnered its treasures. On the flanks of the lower Jordan rested a semitropical garden where the fruits of creation were gathered without regard for the times and seasons restricting husbandmen in other climes. In the distant south rose the soft, brown mountains of Judea where barren Moriah silently anticipated her bedecking as the eternal Jerusalem. Farther on, the Negev watched Bedouin and trader ply the way down to the land of the Pharaohs, ancient Egypt.

It was a unique land for a unique man, one whose life would begin not at the proverbial 40, but at a patriarchal 75. Abraham would be one of a kind, yet he would endure as the spiritual prototype of all believers in Jehovah who would follow after him. In this first Hebrew, the world would witness a fresh phenomenon. A branch was being grafted out of humanity through which the divine purposes would flow; around which all history would revolve; in which all biblical prophecy would one day triumphantly culminate. God was creating a new thing; Jehovah was forming His Israel.

The impact of what occurred in the call of Abraham cannot be lightly passed over — it was not a casual event. Quite literally, it would become the fountainhead of all biblical prescience. Consequently, it would become an essential study for all who aspire to understand history and its most enigmatic element, the Jew.

No people who have left a track upon the face of this sphere have been as consistently conspicuous as the descendents of Abraham. Certainly none have aroused emotions, attracted a greater measure of attention, or made more indelible contributions than have the Jewish people. Why? Why, after all, did God call them? Why did He so obviously set them apart? What did, and does, He intend to show the world through this tiny nation? How is every child of Adam influenced by their presence and Jehovah's program for Israel? The answers to these questions, as we shall see, are intriguing, illuminating, and potentially soul-satisfying.

I Will Bless Thee

In order to properly appraise the full significance of Abraham's place in history, it is necessary to view events from his introduction to us through the biblical record.

Now the LORD had said unto Abram, Get thee
out of thy country, and from thy kindred, and
from thy father's house, unto a land that *I
will* show thee; and *I will* make of thee a great
nation, and *I will* bless thee, and make thy
name great; and thou shalt be a blessing. And
I will bless them that bless thee, and curse
him that curseth thee: and in thee shall all
families of the earth be blessed (Gen. 12:1-3).

Embodied in this initial unveiling of Jehovah's plan for
the future is a fourfold application of *I will*:

1. *I will* show you a land. This involves *divine
direction.*

2. *I will* make thee a great nation. This speaks
of *divine determination.*

3. *I will* bless thee and make thy name great,
and thou shalt be a blessing. Here we see
divine promotion.

4. *I will* bless them that bless thee, and curse
him that curseth thee, and in thee shall all
families of the earth be blessed. This shows
the *divine program.*

These remarkable words were spoken to Abraham, the
childless Shemite, son of an idolater, from the ancient city
of Ur in Mesopotamia. He accepted them by faith and moved
in the appointed direction without knowing his precise
destination. Upon his arrival in the land identified to him
by God, the declarations given earlier were amplified. Three
passages set forth the dimensions of Jehovah's promises.

> And the LORD said unto Abram, after Lot was separated from him, Lift up now thine eyes, and look from the place where thou art northward, and southward, and eastward, and westward, *For all the land which thou seest, to thee will I give it, and to thy seed forever* (Gen. 13:14-15).

> In the same day the LORD made a covenant with Abram, saying, Unto thy seed have I given this land, *from the river of Egypt unto the great river, the river Euphrates* (Gen. 15:18).

> And I will establish my covenant between me and thee and thy seed after thee in their generations for an everlasting covenant, to be a God unto thee, and to thy seed after thee. *And I will give unto thee, and to thy seed after thee, the land wherein thou art a sojourner, all the land of Canaan, for an everlasting possession; and I will be their God* (Gen. 17:7-8).

The magnificent sweep of these prophetic words would prove to be profound and permanently binding, if not immediately realized. A man, childless at 80 years of age, is promised a son. This son, he was told, would become a great nation. The nation was decreed a land by God; it would be theirs forever. Jehovah enters a covenant with the Jewish nation insuring their longevity and national identity as long as history continues. Through the seed of Abraham a Messiah would come to bring blessing and benefit to the entire world!

These declarations were made some 4,000 years ago. If one accepts the Bible as God's instrument of communication to man, he must also quickly acknowledge that the reliability of the biblical account will be tested by whether these promises are faithfully fulfilled. Therefore, the trustworthiness of the message of the Bible is admittedly put to the ultimate trial. Can all of these predictions be fully accomplished over the span of thousands of years? Furthermore, will the results be of a nature that will serve to establish beyond question a literal fulfillment? If this, in fact, comes to pass, it is demonstrably sheer folly, and unbelief of the first order, to propose that the Bible is less than God's revealed Word to man. Also, it will graphically establish the assuring recognition that God is on the scene, moving history toward an orderly culmination.

The Nation

In the course of time Abraham was granted the promised son; the son had a family; the family, in time of famine, moved to Egypt. Under Egyptian bondage the family struggled through the birth pangs of delivering a nation. Some 500 years after those divine proclamations to a lone patriarch in a distant city, a nation of perhaps two or three million souls marched out of Egypt to again occupy the Promised Land.

Israel's exodus from Pharaoh's domain endures as one of the great epochs of all time. Moses contesting with Pharaoh, the successive plagues which rolled over the land, and the miraculous deliverance by their passage through the Red Sea are all familiar events to Jews and Christians. It has been celebrated by Jews in the annual Passover ceremony across the long centuries. Christians revere its memory as one of the great Old Testament previews of the sacrificial work of Christ. Hundreds of novels and historical works have been based upon it. Filmmakers and songwriters have repeatedly used its theme. More recently, it was remembered as Jewish people began making their trek across the face of the nations in the return to Israel after the rebirth of the state.

Israel's deliverance from servitude in Egypt and her subsequent journey through the wilderness would be one of the most productive short periods in history; we are all beneficiaries of these momentous days. During this time the Law was given to Moses, the first five books of the Bible (the Torah) were written, and Moses was established as perhaps the greatest leader of men the world would know.

During the trip from Egypt to Canaan, the Israelites paused for nearly a year before Mount Sinai to receive their unprecedented revelation from God. The priestly ministry was established at this time, and the Tabernacle, the first national house of worship, was built. It was a time of great national optimism. Israel had been favored by a direct communication from God. He had instructed them, through the Law, regarding their religious worship and service. The land of Abraham, Isaac, and Jacob lay before them. To Jewish people of the day, the future seemed aglow with glorious prospects. But, suddenly, God sent a prophetic shiver down the national spine. They were introduced to the principle by which they would occupy the land God had given them: *They must obey Him.* It was true that Canaan had been given to the Hebrew people in perpetuity. But, if they failed in the matter of basic obedience to their Lord, they would experience expulsion from the land made sacred by the hallowed promises of Jehovah.

In the brief span of a section covering a few chapters in the Bible, the entire historical future of the Jewish people is outlined. It is striking in its detail and in the precision with which the factual historical accounts coincide with prophetic predictions. This astounding revelation identifies four distinct periods in the divine program for the Jewish people. *Dispersion, preservation, restoration,* and *reconciliation* would mark the way of Jewry during their national pilgrimage. The sequence is first recorded in Leviticus, then restated in Deuteronomy. These transcending focal points were touched repeatedly by the Old Testament writers who came after Moses. New Testament penmen took up the threads and wove additional patterns into the fabric. Around these four movements all international developments will revolve. From beginning to end, this little nation will be central to all of God's dealings with mankind. In a very real sense, one can only rightly interpret history as he fully reckons with Israel's singular niche in the unfolding drama of global affairs.

We follow the Leviticus and Deuteronomy accounts for our formative glimpse at Israel's prewritten history.

Dispersion

And if ye *will not for all this hearken unto me, but walk contrary unto me,* Then I will walk contrary unto you also in fury; and I, even I, will chastise you seven times for your sins (Lev. 26:27-28).

And I will scatter you among the nations, and will draw out a sword after you; *and your land shall be desolate,* and your cities waste (Lev. 26:33).

And the LORD *shall scatter thee among all people, from the one end of the earth even unto the other;* and there thou shalt serve other gods, which neither thou nor thy fathers have known, even wood and stone. And among these nations shalt thou find no ease, neither shall the sole of thy foot have rest; but the LORD shall give

thee there a trembling heart, and failing of
eyes, and sorrow of mind. And thy life shall
hang in doubt before thee; and thou shalt fear
day and night, and shalt have no assurance
of thy life (Dt. 28:64-66).

Preservation

And yet for all that, when they are in the land
of their enemies, *I will not cast them away,* neither
will I abhor them, to destroy them utterly,
and to break my covenant with them; for I
am the LORD their God (Lev. 26:44).

And it shall come to pass, when all these things
are come upon thee, the blessing and the curse,
which I have set before thee, and thou shalt
call them to mind *among all the nations,* to which
the LORD thy God hath driven thee (Dt. 30:1).

Restoration

Then will *I remember my covenant* with Jacob,
and also my covenant with Isaac, and also my
covenant with Abraham will I remember; and
I will remember the land (Lev. 26:42).

That then the LORD thy God *will turn thy
captivity,* and have compassion upon thee, and
will return and *gather thee from all the nations*
where the LORD thy God hath scattered thee
(Dt. 30:3).

Reconciliation

But I will for their sakes remember the
covenant of their ancestors, whom I brought
forth out of the land of Egypt in the sight
of the nations, *that I might be their God:* I am
the LORD (Lev. 26:45).

> But I will for their sakes remember the covenant of their ancestors, whom I brought forth out of the land of Egypt in the sight of the nations, *that I might be their God*: I am the LORD (Lev. 26:45).
>
> And the LORD thy God will bring thee into the land which thy fathers possessed, and thou shalt possess it; and he will do thee good, and multiply thee above thy fathers. *And the LORD thy God will circumcise thine heart, and the heart of thy seed, to love the LORD thy God with all thine heart, and with all thy soul*, that thou mayest live (Dt. 30:5-6).

The prophet Jeremiah supplies an emphatic summary of the entire process with these words:

> Behold, I will gather them out of all countries, to which I have driven them in mine anger, and in my fury, and in great wrath; and I will bring them again unto this place, and I will cause them to dwell safely; And they shall be my people, and I will be their God; And *I will give them one heart, and one way, that they may fear me forever*, for the good of them, and of their children after them; And I will make an everlasting covenant with them, that I will not turn away from doing them good, but *I will put my fear in their hearts, that they shall not depart from me*. Yea, I will rejoice over them in doing them good, and I will plant them in this land assuredly with my whole heart and with my whole soul (Jer. 32:37-41).

First, only a comparatively few Jewish people went back to Israel at the time of this return — about 50,000 are estimated to have done so. The rest of their brethren chose to remain in more comfortable circumstances in Babylon. The number of people in the land from that time until the destruction of the Temple in 70 A.D. was always a remnant of the nation, not a full representation of the sons of Jacob. Second, the most extensive dispersion of the nation was still in the future. For nearly 2,000 years the Jewish people would be sojourners among the Gentile nations. Their scattering after the Roman scourging of the land would take them farther from the ancient soil than had ever been the case theretofore. Sufferings endured during their wanderings would stand without parallel in the chronology of mankind's existence. Third, Israel as a nation has never been fully reconciled to Jehovah spiritually. There has, it is safe to say, never been a period in history when Israel in her entirety has had "one heart and one way" in adherence to Jehovah's person and program. We may rest assured that final fulfillment awaits a future day. However, we can, at the same time, recognize that the final realization of these aspirations is drawing near, and we are, even now, caught up on the quickening surge of prophetic movement.

A further obvious conclusion rests in the fact that the detail and scope of the foregoing declarations are no less than astonishing. Predictions that the nation would be dispossessed, scattered but preserved through centuries of dispersion, and finally brought back to the ancient soil to be reestablished as a nation would demand that all fair-minded people examine carefully the historic ramifications of the fulfillments of these prophecies. There can be no serious doubt that in the very existence of the Jewish people, and most certainly with the rebirth of the nation of Israel a present reality, we are living in the presence of a miracle

— one which was surely wrought by God as any from the days of the prophets and apostles.

This fact should lead each of us to realize that in the Bible we possess a book which cannot be casually laid aside as just another volume. Also, one is led to the settled conclusion that if the claims of Scripture have current relevance for Israel as a nation, there must be a present message for individuals as well. As we trace the systematic progression of Jehovah's faithfulness to the chosen seed, we shall find equal cause for hope and rejoicing in what He has provided for each of us.

DISPERSION

The Mosque of Omar (Dome of the Rock) occupies the Temple site

Courtesy Israeli Embassy

By the rivers of Babylon, there we sat down, yea, we wept, when we remembered Zion. We hung our harps upon the willows in the midst thereof. For there they that carried us away captive required of us a song; and they that wasted us required of us mirth, saying, Sing us one of the songs of Zion. How shall we sing the LORD's song in a foreign land?

Psalm 137:1-4

CHAPTER TWO

CAST TO THE FOUR WINDS

MERE HUMAN INGENUITY could never begin to produce fictionally so absorbing, emotion-charged, and exhilarating a drama as is being lived out in the story of the Jewish people. It is one of the surpassing episodes to be found in the human experience. From the birth of the nation in the call of Abraham, through the exodus, conquest of Canaan, rule of the judges, and reign of her kings, Israel's early history runs the gamut from combat to tranquility, rebellion to captivity. Stern voices of bold prophets ring across the pages of the Bible as the nation is called to repentance and allegiance to her God. Psalmists sing captivating melodies which will live throughout the ages as the source of strength and inspiration for men the world over. Kings, princes, and queens, good and bad, all add their deeds and voices to the chronicle. But ever it seems, over it all, one hears the persistent footfall of columned hosts as great empires and petty tyrants thrust and parry for possession of the land. This Gentile obsession to take title to Israel and subjugate her people led to periods of turbulence, captivity, and finally the worldwide dispersion of the Jewish people.

As we view this segment of history, two general features must be identified. They might be characterized as preliminary and primary, or the captivities as opposed to the general dispersion of the nation.

Captivities

These were localized experiences during which major segments of the people were taken into other countries for varying periods of time. Later, they were allowed to return and resume official national life once again. The major captivities were related to two nations, Assyria and Babylonia.

Following the death of Israel's third king, Solomon, his son, Rehoboam, initiated a series of repressive measures on the people. He rejected counsel from elders who pleaded for leniency toward his already over-burdened subjects. His intransigence resulted in a division of the kingdom. In 922 B.C. Jeroboam led a successful insurrection that saw the ten northern tribes, thereafter identified as Israel, severed from the southern tribes, Judah and Benjamin.

The Assyrians, under Tiglath-pileser, later invaded Israel and forced the payment of tribute to the Assyrian monarch. The tribute was paid for a short time before Israel and Damascus agreed on a course of mutual resistance to this arrangement. The end result was a new intrusion by Assyria. This engagement brought about the fall of Damascus and the loss of territories by Israel. In addition, Jewish citizens were taken into exile. A later king, Hoshea, joined his predecessor in resisting the payment of tribute, this time turning to Egypt for assistance. Consequently, Shalmaneser V, then ruler of Assyria, moved to besiege Samaria, the northern capital city. Samaria withstood the siege for three years but finally fell before her foes. In 722 B. C. Shalmaneser's successor, Sargon, who participated in the conflict, reported that 27,290 Israelites were taken into captivity at this time. Thus the kingdom of Israel ceased to exist; only Judah remained.

The Assyrians recruited settlers from Babylonia and Syria to move into the region and dwell among the Israelites who remained in the land. Their assimilation with the Jews produced the Samaritan people so hated by the Judeans in the days of the New Testament.

Where Are the Ten Lost Tribes?

Cultists have constructed elaborate systems, and with them deluded many thousands, in supposedly identifying these *lost tribes* variously as Anglo-Saxons, gypsies, or others who accommodate their personal whims or objectives. They then proceed to mutilate the Scriptures by attempting to relate God's promises to Israel to these *lost tribes*. In reality, the majority of the *lost tribes* were never really lost at all. Several relevant observations on this point are in order.

First, we are told that the exiles were transported by their captors to "Halah, and Habor, and Hara, and to the river Gozan" (1 Chr. 5:26). Authorities locate this area near the Euphrates River in the region between southern Turkey and northern Syria, about 200 miles east of the northeast tip of the Mediterranean Sea. The obvious conclusion regarding them is that they remained there until the Assyrian power was broken by the Babylonians and then returned to their homes in Israel or stayed put, as they chose.

Next we have documentation that a great many Israelites remained in the land and never left it at all. During the revival under Hezekiah, king of Judah, it is stated that the king sent invitations to the northern tribes "from Beer-sheba even to Dan, that they should come to keep the Passover unto the LORD God of Israel at Jerusalem" (2 Chr. 30:5).

Favorable responses were received from members of five of the tribes of Israel: Asher, Manasseh, Zebulun, Ephraim, and Issachar. The passage indicates that a large number of Israelites came to join the Judeans for the Passover celebration at Jerusalem.

A further conclusion is that many pious Jews would most certainly eventually migrate south as the foreign elements, which had been sent in by the Assyrians, brought in oppressive pagan practices and influences. It would be Jews from all branches of Jacob's posterity, men of faith, believers in the promises of Jehovah, who would identify with the worship of the Temple and the place of the Davidic throne. We can, therefore, rest assured that all of Israel is represented in present-day Jewry, and we need not search further for those ten lost tribes.

Judeans, although having escaped the Assyrian scourge, would also share the fate of their northern brothers. Judah's impending trial was predicted 150 years before it took place.

> Be in pain, and labor to bring forth, O daughter of Zion, like a woman in travail; for now shalt thou go forth out of the city, and thou shalt dwell in the field, and thou shalt go even to Babylon; there shalt thou be delivered; there the LORD shall redeem thee from the hand of thine enemies (Mic. 4:10).

Jeremiah foretold the duration of the captivity.

> And this whole land shall be a desolation, and an horror; and these nations shall serve the king of Babylon seventy years (Jer. 25:11).

As the prophet predicted, Babylon did indeed annex Judah. In 586 B.C. Jerusalem was sacked and the magnificent Temple of Solomon pillaged and put to the torch. The first confirmed physical evidence of this destruction by Nebuchadnezzar was discovered by Israeli archaeologists during the 1975 digging season. Professor Nathan Avigad unearthed four bronze and iron arrowheads of Babylonian origin at the base of a defense tower in the Jewish quarter of the Old City.

As the year 605 B.C. began, Egypt was in control of Israel and Syria. This condition would no longer endure. The Babylonians, led by Nebuchadnezzar, fell to Pharaoh-neco and his forces at Carchemish. He dealt them a defeat which broke the power of Egypt and left the way to Syria and Israel open to the victors. An advance was made into Judah, resulting in Jehoiakim, then the reigning sovereign, being forced to agree to tribute payments to Nebuchadnezzar. Later, Jehoiakim refused to honor his pledge and consequently fell prey to Babylonian wrath. Although the king's life was spared, which in itself was a minor miracle, the Temple was sacked and a number of captives taken to Babylon. Among those making the long journey into exile were Daniel, Shadrach, Meshach, and Abednego.

Eleven years later, in 597 B.C., Israel would learn another lesson in the cost of rebellion. On this occasion the emissaries of Nebuchadnezzar placed Jerusalem under siege. The city fell on August 1, 586 B.C. In an attempt to instill an attitude of enduring subservience in the Jewish mind, the king ordered the Temple devastated and its valuables removed. The city and the king's palace were burned. Except for the nondescript, the citizens were taken into captivity.

Judeans mounted one more futile uprising in 581 B.C. The end result was the same. For the third time Jews were carried off the Judean hills away to the banks of the Chebar. Some Israelites, however, fled to Egypt rather than become captives. Jeremiah the prophet chose this course of action.

And so the prophetic word was served once again. For 70 years the Hebrews labored in a strange land. They wept by the river of Babylon, raised their lament, and longed to see beloved Jerusalem once more.

At the close of the appointed years, godly Jews seized the opportunity to return to their homes. By 516 B.C. the Temple was reconstructed by the eager hands of those who had joined the first wave of returnees.

In 538 B.C. the Persians swept aside the Babylonians and became entrenched as the power to reckon with. Their leader, Cyrus, granted the Jews leave to return to the land, and Zerubbabel led a small group back to the homeland. Ezra the scribe led another band out in 457 B.C. (about 6,000 were numbered in this host). Thirteen years later, Nehemiah led yet another assembly of travelers on the rigorous trek back to the land.

Actually, comparatively few of the people returned to Israel at this time. They had known a great measure of freedom and prosperity in the land of their conquerors. Consequently, many chose to remain rather than face the dangers of the way and the uncertainties awaiting them. Estimates of the number of people in the Jewish community during the time of Nehemiah is set at approximately 125,000. These people composed the remnant which shared the vigil through the long years of waiting for the appearance of the promised Messiah.

It should be noted that with the Babylonian conquest of Judah, a period of Gentile denomination of Israel began which continued virtually unbroken until very recent days.

The Mystery of the Missing Ark

The Ark of the Covenant was the central piece of furniture in the Temple of Solomon. It had, in fact, been at the heart of Jewish worship since the Mosaic system was introduced at Mount Sinai. Moses received instructions for its dimensions and order of construction directly from Jehovah. The Ark was a chest, 3¾ feet in length by 2¼ feet wide and high. It was made of acacia wood covered within and without by gold. Inside were the two tables of the Decalogue. It was from above this Ark, between the covering cherubim attached to the Mercy Seat which rested upon the Ark, that Jehovah communed with Israel.

> And there I will meet with thee, and I will commune with thee from above the mercy seat, from between the two cherubim which are upon the ark of the testimony, of all things which I will give thee in commandment unto the children of Israel (Ex. 25:22).

Before the Ark the high priest entered once each year to make an offering for the people and accomplish atonement for their sins.

With the Babylonian destruction of the Temple, the Ark dropped from view. All considerations of its fate must be confined to the speculative, because we lack conclusive information from which to proceed. Several possibilities have been suggested.

Possibly, it was destroyed by the marauding Babylonians who would have been interested in salvaging the gold it contained. It could have been taken back to Babylon as a trophy of war. There is, however, no mention of its being among the valuables described in the listing of confiscated items in 2 Kings 25.

A rabbinical tradition asserts it was buried at some point under the Temple Mount by priests before the Babylonians captured the city. If this were true, it would still be there, as we well know it has never been unearthed. There is strong sentiment today among some high-ranking rabbis in favor of this view. It is their contention that the Ark is indeed buried beneath the Mount and will yet be found.

Still another tradition is contained in one of the apocryphal books which attributes the removal of the Ark from Jerusalem to Jeremiah.

> It was also contained in the same writing, that the prophet, being warned of God, commanded the tabernacle and the ark to go with him, as he went forth into the mountain, where Moses climbed up and saw the heritage of God. And when Jeremy came thither, he found an hollow cave, wherein he laid the tabernacle, and the ark, and the altar of incense, and so stopped the door (2 Macc. 2:4-5).

This account proceeds to say the cave location was lost and awaits disclosure by the Lord at some later date.

Others believe the Ark to have been transported to Heaven where it now rests. Support for this view is claimed from Revelation 11:19. Here John describes his look into the heavenly Temple. "And the temple of God was opened in heaven, and there was seen in his temple the ark of his covenant." The question is whether this is the actual Ark known to Israel or a heavenly version which occupies the celestial Temple.

Dr. Benjamin Mazar, who is in charge of all excavations in Jerusalem, does not believe the Ark to be in existence. He feels that if it were not destroyed, it would have long since decayed and disintegrated. This view, however, does not take into account the fact that the wood was encased in gold and contained stone articles. He does concede that were he and his associates to discover the Ark, it would have a most dramatic effect on the nation and, for that matter, the world.

It most assuredly would! Finding the Ark would rank with the resurrection of the nation Israel and the reunification of Jerusalem as a landmark in Jewish history. In many respects it would certainly surpass even these illustrious events. The prophetic implications of such a find would be equally monumental. The immediate reaction from Jews the world over would be for a proper house for its most unique national treasure. The only acceptable resting place, of course, would be a new Temple. This possibility illustrates the dramatic swiftness with which great events could unfold before us in these last days.

It is noteworthy that Jeremiah mentions the lack of necessity for an Ark in the ultimate future of Israel.

> And it shall come to pass, when ye are multiplied and increased in the land, in those days, saith the LORD, they shall say no more, The ark of the covenant of the LORD, neither shall it come to mind, neither shall they remember it, neither shall they miss it, neither shall that be done any more (Jer. 3:16).

Also, the millennial Temple description in Ezekiel 40-44 makes no mention of it, and for good reason. In that glorious day our reigning Messiah-Savior, Jesus Christ, will be light, law, redemption, and righteousness. There will be no further need for a symbol when He appears on the scene!

The General Dispersion

Preparation for the final dispersion dawned with Roman domination of the land. Until the Roman period, the armies of a succession of foreign rulers made themselves felt among the people. Following the Babylonians came the Medes and the Persians. In their wake entered the swift forces of

Alexander the Great. Finally, the Romans wrested control of the strip of land that could never repose comfortably under any Gentile foot. This unwelcome and uneasy yoke prevailed at Christ's birth.

The Words of Jesus

The great light of the coming expulsion of the Jews from Palestine was given by Jesus Christ in the Gospel records of the New Testament. As we have seen, a large number of Jewish people were already dwelling in other countries. Such famous Jewish communities as those in Alexandria, Egypt, and Babylon had long been well-known and were vying with the Jews in Israel for theological supremacy. The great feasts were swollen by large numbers of Israelites from far-off nations who assembled for brief spiritual respite within the environs of the sacred Temple Mount.

Jesus predicted some 40 years before it occurred the destruction of the Temple and the siege and fall of the city of Jerusalem.

> As for these things which ye behold, the days will come, in which *there shall not be left one stone upon another, that shall not be thrown down* (Lk. 21:6).

> And when ye shall see Jerusalem compassed with armies, then know that its desolation is near. Then let them who are in Judea flee to the mountains; and let them who are in the midst of it depart; and let not them that are in the countries enter into it. For these are the days of vengeance, that all things which are written may be fulfilled. But woe unto them that are with child, and to them that nurse children, in those days! For there shall

be great distress in the land, and wrath upon this people. And they shall fall by the edge of the sword, *and shall be led away captive into all nations; and Jerusalem shall be trodden down by the Gentiles, until the times of the Gentiles be fulfilled* (Lk. 21:20-24).

Christ's prophecy embodies three assertions:

1. The Temple would be destroyed.
2. The nation would be dispersed and Jerusalem come under Gentile domination until Israel returned to the land.
3. The time of Gentile world ascendancy would come to a close.

Destruction

There shall not be left one stone upon another.

The disciples were thunderstruck by Christ's statement concerning the Temple. This magnificent edifice graced the crown of Mount Moriah in Jerusalem. All of Jewish life, in and out of Israel, revolved around this building. ·

The Temple, built by Herod the Great, had been under construction in excess of 40 years and was still some 40 years from completion. It was the wonder of the religious world. The white marble and richly ornamented gold seemed at times to fairly illuminate the city. As visiting pilgrims approached the outskirts, the Temple suddenly came into view gleaming in the sunlight against the cool green backdrop of the Mount of Olives. The ancient historian, Josephus, provides a vivid description of the scene.

Viewed from without, the Sanctuary had everything that could amaze either mind or eyes. Overlaid all around with stout plates of gold, in the first rays of the sun it reflected so fierce a blaze of fire that those who endeavored to look at it were forced to turn away as if they had looked straight at the sun. To strangers as they approached it seemed in the distance like a mountain covered with snow; for any part not covered with gold was dazzling white.

It seemed inconceivable to the disciples that the Temple would ever be destroyed. Yet this was the Lord's prophecy, and in 70 A.D. His stunning words were graphically fulfilled.

By 66 A.D. Jewish discontent had fomented into open rebellion against Rome. The final straw was dropped by one Gessius Florus, procurator of Judea, who chose a course of cruel repression of the rebellious Jews. His undoing was a raid on the Temple in Jerusalem, the removal of funds, and a massacre of many inhabitants of the city. The inevitable contest was thus initiated.

After a brief series of attempts at reconciliation and military skirmishing, the full weight of the Roman colossus began to rumble toward Israel. Rome's choice for the command over the advancing legionnaires was Vespasian, the finest human weapon in the imperial arsenal. He mounted a systematic campaign carefully crafted to demonstrate emphatically the folly of ambitions toward independence. The final result of his grand object lesson remained visible throughout history. Shortly before the last desperate struggle for the city, Vespasian left the field to follow his fortunes to Rome in quest of becoming emperor. He succeeded and dispatched his son Titus to pursue the grim business of placing Jerusalem under siege.

In August of 70 A.D. the hammer fell on the beleaguered Jews. Of course, they never actually had a chance to succeed in deposing their overlord. Yet their tenacity and valor through the hopeless contest must stand as one of the most arresting chapters in the annals of military history.

The siege was brought to an end as the legions breached the walls and slowly penetrated into the city. After severe and protracted street fighting, they reached the Temple itself. During the deadly struggle, fire broke out in the hallowed sanctuary, and soon the cedar beams and roof were spewing flame and smoke. The very heart of Judaism was being torn from its breast.

By the time the triumphant legionnaries paraded through the streets of Rome bearing on their shoulders the sacred vessels of Jewish worship, the words of Christ had been lived out in minute detail. There was literally not one stone left upon another. As the conflagration ran its course, the precious metals which adorned the walls ran down between the giant marble blocks — some of which were nearly 70 feet long by nine feet in width. The bands of plunderers responded by methodically removing the blocks in order to retrieve the coveted treasure. The destruction was soon complete.

Desolation

...and shall be led away captive into all nations.

Without a sanctuary and with beloved Jerusalem firmly in the grasp of the Gentile adversary, the Jewish people began their two thousand-year trek across the pages of history. After the fall of Jerusalem, multitudes of Jews were taken into captivity.

The final humiliation, however, came when they rallied to the side of Bar Kochba in 132 A.D. This effort was their last fling at liberation. The final uprising was precipitated when the Emperor Hadrian, who visited Judea in 130 A.D., decided to rebuild Jerusalem, and, in the process, change its name. He further proposed to build a shrine to the god Zeus on the Temple site. The Jews were further incensed at his decrees which proscribed circumcision and the observance of the Sabbath.

Bar Kochba, *Son of a Star,* offered himself as a military messiah who would banish their adversary's Goliath and win lasting freedom. He conducted a guerrilla-type campaign which met with initial success. Jerusalem was taken and named as capital and religious center of the new regime. The optimistic leader even minted coins with the inscription "For the freedom of Jerusalem." These coins were dated "Year One," "Year Two," "Year Three." There was to be no "Year Four." Rome savagely retaliated and, as a result, both combatants suffered enormous losses. Bar Kochba was slain and the insurrection shattered. Jerusalem and its people once again awaited Roman retribution. It was both swift and severe. The city was again leveled to the ground. This time the Temple Mount was put to the plow. Jews were banished from the city and its environs and were forbidden to enter for the next 200 years. Any person attempting to return and repair houses was to be executed.

Roman vengeance was not confined to the city of David. Olive groves for miles around were cut down. Galilee, noted for its olive production, had scarcely a tree left standing. Villages were burned. For a time a scorched-earth policy was rigidly enforced. Slave markets were set up at Gaza and Hebron, and, as the words of Christ had predicted, auctioneers sold Jews to foreign slavers who carried them to the far reaches of the world. Others, who had escaped the tyrant's grasp, packed tattered belongings and slipped quietly out of the land to begin the long centuries of enforced exile.

A new Roman city, Aelia Capitolina, now took the place of Jewish Jerusalem. In its midst stood the objects which were perhaps the most symbolically illustrative elements in the entire, dreadful scene. They were the statue of the Emperor Hadrian and a shrine to the Roman god Jupiter that stood on the Temple Mount over the spot to which Jews had come from every corner of the earth to worship Jehovah.

In closing this section, it will be well for us to ponder the fact that the leadership who had examined and rejected the messianic credentials of the Prince of Peace were willing to follow a usurper who strapped on a sword. The relative results of the lives of both bear irrefutable testimony as to whose claims were genuine.

PRESERVATION

Siege ramp built by the Romans at Masada, 70-73 A.D.
Courtesy Israeli Embassy

Masada — where 960 Jews died following the fall of Jerusalem, 70 A.D.
Courtesy Israeli Embassy

I will send a faintness into their hearts in the lands of their enemies, and the sound of a shaken leaf shall chase them; and they shall flee, as fleeing from a sword; and they shall fall when none pursueth.
Leviticus 26:36

CHAPTER THREE

THE LONG, LONELY ROAD

THE LONG-STANDING PROMISES to Moses in Leviticus would now be tested to the fullest possible extent. "And yet for all that, when they are in the land of their enemies, I will not cast them away" (Lev. 26:44). Amazing words! A numerically insignificant people were to be dispossessed from their homeland, dispersed among the nations, experience the intermittent hatred of the peoples among whom they would settle, have no Temple to preserve religious continuity, and remain in this condition for nearly two thousand years. With these facts in view, the prediction by the ancient prophet would necessitate one of two possibilities. Either the prognosticator was mentally unhinged, or he had some *inside information*. To attempt an explanation along with the lines of a wild guess theory is not worth serious consideration.

Universally, the inspired penman struck bold assertions as to the preservation of the Jews as a national entity during the coming displacement. These are not shrouded, vague references, but bold, clear, repeated predictions which place the reliability of the biblical record squarely on the line.

A passage from Jeremiah will illustrate the point:

> Thus saith the LORD, who giveth the sun for a light by day, and the ordinances of the moon and of the stars for a light by night, who divideth the sea when its waves roar; The LORD of hosts is his name: *If those ordinances depart from before me, saith the LORD, then the seed of Israel also shall cease from being a nation before me forever. Thus saith the LORD, If heaven above can be measured, and the foundations of the earth searched out beneath, I will also cast off all the seed of Israel for all that they have done, saith the LORD* (Jer. 31:35-37).

How dogmatic is the writer about the matter of Jewish preservation? If the sun can be extinguished! If the moon can be prevented from influencing the tides! If the stars can somehow be caused to flicker and die! If we can successfully measure the expanse of space about us! If all of the mysteries of the earth can be solved! *"I will also cast off all the seed of Israel."*

No one in his right mind would venture such statements unless he in truth possessed *inside information.* History has unequivocally demonstrated that *he did.* The God of history provided the prophet with the information hundreds of years before it was lived out on the stage of human events. There is no other possibility.

Jews have been tracked, slaughtered, maligned, and driven from nation to nation over the centuries. There is no depth of human resourcefulness which can account for the fact that they are still with us as a nation. The only acceptable explanation for Jewry's tenacious refusal to lie down and die is actual divine preservation coupled with a divinely induced infusion of desire to survive.

The Wandering Jew

Most of us are at least vaguely familiar with the appellation, "The Wandering Jew." It has been bestowed upon a card game and a game of dice. Plants and birds have also borne the title. The principal recipients, however, are the sons of Abraham, who through this caricatured legend are pictured in their wanderings during the long years of the dispersion.

The first written record of the Wandering Jew comes down to us from the 13th century. It alleges that a Jew in Armenia had been found who had been a personal witness to the sufferings of Christ. He had shouted at Jesus, "Go, thou tempter and seducer, to receive what you have earned." The Lord is said to have replied, "I go and you will await me until I come again." Thus the Jew was condemned to wander the earth until the second advent of Christ.

All stories of this legendary figure are essentially the same as the one related above. Perhaps the most universally represented is one which came from Germany in the year 1602.

> ...it is related that Paulus Von Eitzen, bishop of Schleswig, in the winter of 1542, when attending church in Hamburg, saw a tall man, dressed in threadbare garments, with long hair, standing barefoot in the chancel; whenever the name of Jesus was pronounced he bowed his head, beat his breast, and sighed profoundly. It was reported that he was a shoemaker named Ahasuerus who had cursed Jesus on his way to the crucifixion. On further questioning he related the historical events that had taken place since. He conversed in the language of the country he happened to

be visiting. This version shows "Ahasuerus" was a fully fledged personification of the Jewish people, incorporating the themes of participation of the crucifixion, condemnation to eternal suffering until Jesus' second coming, and the bearing witness to the truth of the Christian tradition. The description of the person suggests the well-known figure of the Jewish peddler.[1]

And so the tone is set with the Jewish people portrayed as perpetual wanderers among the nations of the world. While there may seem, to some, to be rather quaint aspects to this fanciful generalization of the Jewish condition, there would be nothing quaint about what Jews were to experience at the hands of the Gentiles during the years of their pilgrimage.

INSTRUMENTS OF TERROR

Footsteps in a darkened hallway or a sudden knock on the door have historically brought a very real cause for apprehension for Jewish people in many parts of the world. The catalog of satanic instruments fashioned to bring them pain and humiliation is almost beyond human power of description. The sheer ingenuity and persistent reapplication of some of these instruments of terror lay bare a clear conspiracy of evil with which we might all do well to familiarize ourselves. As unpleasant as some of these things are to remember, it will be seen, even today, that too many of them linger still. In the light of current developments and the possible trend toward a new wave of militant anti-Semitism, we should all be aware of these devices by which we are apt to be confronted.

Pogroms

A small Jewish family shared a simple evening meal together in their home in Odessa, Russia. The year was 1905. For some weeks political turmoil had provided the central topic of conversation throughout the town. Much of the talk carried threatening overtones. News had filtered in of attacks which had been made on Jews in surrounding communities. The youthful husband attempted to avoid communicating his inner fears to his wife and two small children. Suddenly, the clatter of horses' hoofs sounded across the yard. He sprang toward the door through which the gruff voices of the booted intruders were now clearly audible. Without so much as a command to allow them inside, the door was battered in. The husband's short-lived effort to protect his family proved pitifully inadequate. He was cut down with a single sword thrust. The terror-stricken mother was torn from the desperate grasp of her children and forced through a door into another room by several bearded ruffians. The children's demise would be painful but quick when compared to the protracted torment of their dying mother. The ordeal ended as the cruel intruders loaded up the humble belongings of the family and moved on to other conquests. Before the work was completed, 300 Jews were dispatched, while thousands of others escaped with wounds which would serve as lifelong memorials of the infamous event.

The Pogrom was originated in Russia and is, by definition, an attack. It is a swift, localized form of brutality which has as its major ingredients looting, destruction, rape, and murder. Pogroms were carried out extensively in Russia between 1881 and 1921. They were not confined to Russia, but were also a weapon employed by anti-Semitic movements in Germany, Rumania, Austria, the Balkans, Morocco, Algeria, Persia, and other areas. In Russia alone, during the years of the Civil War, 1,236 such attacks are known to have taken place. The result was an estimated 60,000 dead and many more wounded.

Expulsions

Of more general and far-reaching consequences were the periodic expulsions from various cities and countries. We have touched on the expulsions of Jews from Israel by the ancient empires, Assyria and Rome. Rome further afflicted them by periodically expelling all Jewish people from the capital city. In 19 A.D., for example, Tiberius ordered all Jews who would not renounce their faith to leave Rome.

Expulsions from localities were extended for various periods of time and for a number of reasons. During the 15th and 16th centuries Jews were frequently put out of towns in Germany and northern Italy. Naples, Prague, Genoa, the Papal State (Italy), Moscow, and Vienna were among the localities which bear the distinction of having sent the Jews packing at some time in their history. The years of the plague, remembered as the Black Death (1348-50), which swept Europe saw Jews accused as being responsible for the presence of the disease. They were said to be guilty of poisoning wells and other water sources with infectious elements. As a result, many were massacred and banished from regions in Spain, France, Germany, and Austria.

Fourteen hundred ninety-two is celebrated by Americans as the year in which a Genoese sailor, Christopher Columbus, discovered our great land. It is also enshrined in the memories of the Jewish people, but for quite another reason. It was in 1492 that Ferdinand and Isabella, the Spanish monarchs, decreed that Jews should be exiled from Spain. This proved to be a severe blow to Jewish residents who had prospered greatly and, in the process, contributed significantly to the betterment of life in Spain. It is estimated that at this time there were more Jewish people residing in Spain than anywhere else in Europe. It was a disastrous epoch for Abraham's posterity in other areas as well. Between 1492 and 1497 they were also denied a place in Sicily, Lithuania, and Portugal. These expulsions followed on the heels of enforced exiles from England (1290) and France (1306 and 1394). Consequently, for some time after 1492 there were no acknowledged Jews living on the European coast of the Atlantic Ocean, which was during this time the center of world trade.

Other instances could be cited which inflicted a variety of miseries on the People of the Book. They suffered from forced sales, confiscated properties, and severe losses from being forced to leave behind uncollectible debts. Disease, hunger, and the ever-present danger of falling prey to ruthless highwaymen became allies of the former tormentors to plague the unwilling migrants. A vivid description of their miseries has been preserved. The comment is from a victim of the expulsion from Spain.

> We ate the grass of the fields, and every day
> I ground with my own hands in the house
> of the Ishmaelites for the thinnest slice of bread
> not even fit for a dog. During the nights, my
> stomach was close to the ground — and my
> belly my cushion. Because of the great cold
> of the autumn — we had no garments in the
> frost and no houses to lodge in — we dug
> trenches in the refuse heaps in the town and
> put our bodies therein.[2]

Jewry was a fluid entity during those unsettled years of searching for a place of security, one to call home. The solemn words of Moses fall again upon our minds: "And among these nations shalt thou find no ease, neither shall the sole of thy foot have rest; but the LORD shall give thee there a trembling heart, and failing of eyes, and sorrow of mind" (Dt. 28:65).

Blood Libels

This preposterous allegation has ranged the globe from ancient days to modern times. It has risen repeatedly to afflict the Jewish people. It embodies the accusation of ritual human sacrifice, using human blood for the Passover ceremony, and cannibalism. It is believed the blood libel was employed by the infamous Antiochus Epiphanes as a pretext upon which to justify his profanation of the Temple.

Although these allegations were repeatedly documented as falsehoods, and so declared by prominent persons including an emperor and a pope, it was too convenient a tool of destruction to be laid aside. We do not know how many Jewish people have suffered and died because of the fiction of the blood libel, but we do know it was used regularly by anti-Semitic elements in Russia as late as the 1870's. The most terrifying example of its destructive evil is witnessed in Hitler's unabashed use of it against hapless European Jewry during the Holocaust.

Protocols of the Elders of Zion

Many readers of these pages will have viewed some form of this document. It accuses an elite element, the Elders of Zion, of joining in a clandestine effort to take over the world by controlling finances and dominating key political positions in various countries of the world. It is interesting to observe that the people who rail on the Jews for their involvement in banking and address themselves to the lurking Jewish conspiracy they say this evidences are the same types who, in the Middle Ages, literally forced Jews into lending by refusing to allow them to sustain a livelihood by any other means. It is well known that the church had proscribed usury (lending money at interest) for its members. Jews, therefore, were allowed to practice what good Christians could not. So they became financiers from whom Christians borrowed and whom they later disliked because of the profits derived from the practice. These protocols, along with the blood libel, have been repeatedly repudiated by Jews and responsible Gentiles as well. Nicholas II of Russia, although himself anti-Semitic, went on record as branding the version given him as being absurd. The most recent popular version is believed to have been written by a member of the Russian secret police in the hope of influencing the Russian Czar mentioned above. The writer adapted his version from a French political pamphlet by one Maurice Joyly in which the ambitions for world domination by Napoleon III are given. The Russian made the transfer to the Jews and proceeded from that point.

Many have credulously adopted the protocols as justification for being anti-Semitic. At one period Henry Ford, Sr. sponsored this view in the United States. It was used with telling effect by Russian opponents of Jews; and, of course, Adolf Hitler and his Nazis used it as a basis for their rationale in the attempt to liquidate the nation in exile.

Currently, it is being turned against political Zionism as justification for the proposed dismemberment of the state of Israel. Egypt's Nasser took this tack, which has been applauded by many who are attempting to promote a schism between "Jews" and "Zionists" who, they say, are only interested in expansionism and ultimate domination of the Middle East.

The Badge

Jews have been marked for persecution most visibly by the forced wearing of given types of apparel. In the Middle Ages they were subjected to such humiliations as wearing pointed hats (in the Germanic countries). In England Jews were forced to wear a distinguishing badge — Henry III enforced this practice. Edward I decreed it should be yellow and larger than previously required. In France a circular emblem was the fashion at one period. It was either to be yellow or red and white. Some localities required it to be worn on both front and back. All Jews, beginning as early as age seven, were forced to display it on their persons. In Spain it was called "the Badge of Shame." The order there was not enforced as consistently as in other areas. Fredrick II ordered all Jewish people in the Kingdom of Sicily to wear a blue badge in the shape of the Greek letter T. Men were also forced to wear beards as a further means of identification. In Rome in 1360 it was a red cape for men and red aprons for the women.

These badges, hats, capes, scarves, aprons, and other devices were used at given intervals over an extended period of time. The reason was exclusive: It said, *This is a Jew*. The most devastating consequence of being thus identified was during World War II, when European Jewry wore on their chests the yellow patch shaped in the form of the Star of David. It was affixed to them as a prelude to their march to the gas chambers.

The Ghetto

This instrument was created in order to pen up Jews in preassigned geographical areas. It was born in the Church Councils of the Middle Ages when decisions were made prohibiting Jews and Christians from living together. It appeared as a permanent institution in Venice in 1516 when Jews "who sought refuge in the city, from which they had been excluded for a lengthy period, were admitted on the condition that they live in a designated quarter, an isolated island among the canals of Venice which could easily be completely cut off from its surroundings by a wall, gates and drawbridges."[3] This became the established pattern by which the ghetto was distinguished: walled enclosures with gates which could be closed if desired. Some were laid out with only one gate which could be guarded at night in order to prevent Jews from leaving the area. Ghettos were to be found in both Christian and Muslim countries in the Middle Ages and later. None, however, equalled the inhumane barbarities of the infamous Warsaw Ghetto of the Holocaust.

The Crusades

One of the most lamentable periods in the annals of Jewish-Christian history was the Crusades, which saw successive waves of mail-clad armies move across Europe on the march to deliver the Holy Sepulcher from the Saracean infidels. The idea was to establish a Christian kingdom in Palestine. Although there were, no doubt, many sincere and devout individuals involved in these adventurous excursions, the practical results were in many respects most regrettable.

Bands of crusaders attacked Jewish sectors in German and French towns on the way to the Middle East. Many Jews were massacred. The culmination came with the fall of Jerusalem on July 15, 1099. No mantle of chivalrous romanticism can obscure the grim specter of death standing over the scene that day. The city was literally filled with the bodies of those slain by the invaders. Jews were burned alive in their synagogues and slaughtered in the temple area. By a participant's own account, "They cut down with the sword every one whom they found in Jerusalem, and spared no one. The victors were covered with blood from head to foot."[4] The Jews have never forgotten.

The Holocaust

No period in all of the suffering of Jewry can equal the singular enormity of the savage attempt to liquidate European Jewry during World War II. Adolf Hitler's demonical "final solution to the Jewish problem" will endure as the darkest hour in Jewish history over the two millennia of the dispersion.

Efforts to begin to provide some dim glimpse of this era will most certainly prove futile. Perhaps the most documentation one can examine — although statistics, too, in this case are admittedly inadequate — is a visual estimate of the human toll exacted from a decimated people.

Polish-Soviet Area	4,565,000
Germany	125,000
Austria	65,000
Czechoslovakia	277,000
Hungary, including northern Transylvania	402,000
France	83,000
Belgium	24,000
Luxembourg	700
Italy	7,500
The Netherlands	106,000
Norway	760
Rumania	40,000
Yugoslavia	60,000
Greece	65,000
Total Jews liquidated	**5,820,960**

And so the pathetic sobs of suffering Jewry rise from the pages of history. Pagans, Muslims, Christians, and atheists have all joined in the flagellation of the Chosen People. It is indeed a painful fact to contemplate, but there it is, etched in blood, chiseled forever in the granite of the historical tablets. Yet, above the staccato of man's frenzied efforts to extinguish the Jew, rise the deep, resounding tones of the eternal Word of God, "And yet for all that, when they are in the land of their enemies, *I will not cast them away,* neither will I abhor them, to destroy them utterly, and to break my covenant with them; for I am the LORD their God" (Lev. 26:44).

As one surveys the sordid catalog of debilitating destructiveness unleashed against the Jewish people over the centuries, he is first stunned by the knowledge of man's capacity to afflict fellow human beings. Then the searching query rises: Why, after all of this, do Jews choose to retain their identity? Would it not have been more prudent for them to have quietly slipped away into the anonymity of assimilation? After all, this is precisely what has occurred in the cases of numbers of Israel's ancient contemporaries. Where are the Hittites, Hivites, Jebusites, and a host of other nations of Bible days? They have long since experienced assimilation and are now all but forgotten to us. Only occasionally do historians study their place in history. Archaeologists examine physical evidences of their passing tenure in the Middle East, but, in fact, these people have been lost as identifiable entities.

Not so with Israel. They have endured, endured through wearying centuries as great world powers rose, declined, and then lapsed into the musty recesses of memory. It can only be emphatically restated: The Jews are a miracle people, a people whose story defies analysis apart from divine revelation. Historians and anthropologists have long bent their minds to the task of explaining the Jewish people. They cannot! How do you explain a people who have survived systematic vilification and persecution while scattered among the world as a nation without a flag, country, or capital, a people who were given no flickering ray of assurance from any human source that they would again occupy fully the land from which they had been expelled?

The People of Promise

There is but one explanation for the perseverance of the Jew: *God keeps His word.* Whatever mysteries rest beyond the grasp of finite minds, one thing is sure: A God who has pledged Himself to the continuity of this people has been faithful to His promise. This being unchallengeably true, it will refresh us to pause for some reflection on the biblical foundations upon which Israel's assurance reposes.

Divine Love

Jehovah assures Israel, through the Prophet Isaiah, that His love for the sons and daughters of Jacob is real. "Since thou wast precious in my sight, thou hast been honorable, and I have loved thee; therefore will I give men for thee, and people for thy life" (Isa. 43:4). He further reveals that His purpose in the establishment of Israel is that this people who "are called by my name and created for my glory" might reflect Jehovah's love to an errant world. God himself provides the explanation: "For thou are an holy people unto the LORD thy God; the LORD thy God hath chosen thee to be a special people unto himself, above all the people who are upon the face of the earth" (Dt. 7:6).

Divine Loyalty

Further amplification comes to us as God reveals that this love is not vested in fluctuating emotional whims but is constant in its loyalty. "The LORD did not set his love upon you, nor choose you, because ye were more in number than any people; for ye were the fewest of all people. But because the LORD loved you, and because he would keep the oath which he had sworn unto your fathers, hath the LORD brought you out with a mighty hand, and redeemed you out of the house of bondage, from the hand of Pharaoh, king of Egypt" (Dt. 7:7-8). In other words, not one of the promises established through the great covenant transactions between Jehovah, Abraham, and his posterity will fail. As Israel was delivered out of the suffering and bondage of Egypt by the hand of God, so she shall be delivered from every evil design set against her by contemporary enemies. The fact is, Israel will not only endure but will one day, as we shall find, emerge totally triumphant with every God-given promise fully delivered.

Divine Longing

At the base of the divine program for the Chosen People is the desire for the full establishment of all He has designed for Israel to be and do. The Lord will only be fully satisfied when His people are fully devoted to Him. Even during those dark hours of distress when the Jewish people have questioned God's interest or very presence, His resolve has remained unshaken. "But Zion said, The LORD hath forsaken me, and my Lord hath forgotten me. Can a woman forget her nursing child, that she should not have compassion on the son of her womb? Yea, they may forget, yet will I not forget thee. Behold, I have engraved thee upon the palms of my hands; thy walls are continually before me" (Isa. 49:14-16). Divine longing consummates in that yet future day when all of the processes which have run their course through the earthly experience of the nation Israel will bring about full national reconciliation and God's faithful word will be accomplished: "And they shall be my people, and I will be their God; And I will give them one heart, and one way, that they may fear me forever, for the good of them, and of their children after them" (Jer. 32:38-39).

Who taught you tender Bible tales
    Of honey land, of milk and wine?
Of peaceful, happy Palestine?
    Of Jordan's holy harvest vales?
Who gave the patient Christ? I say,
    Who gave the Christian creed? Yea, yea,
Who gave your very God to you?
    Your Jew! Your Jew! Your hated Jew!

Joaquin Miller

CHAPTER FOUR

THEN THERE ARE CHRISTIANS

WE MUST FRANKLY ACKNOWLEDGE the fact that much of the persecution falling upon the Jewish people, particularly in Europe, was inflicted by those who were professed followers of Jesus Christ. The Christianized Roman Empire made persecution of Jews official policy. Sword-wielding Christian Crusaders hunted them down. Jews were branded as "Christ killers" by the papacy and consistently hounded in the name of the Church. As important a figure in Protestantism as Martin Luther adopted a strongly anti-Jewish stance. In 1543 he published two books denouncing them. He went so far as to encourage their expulsion, forbid distribution of their books, and advocate the burning of synagogues.

The enduring residual effect has been a deep-seated resentment and suspicion toward Christianity by Jews. Jewish people are well acquainted with what has been done *to them* in the name of Christ so much so that they do not fully recognize what He has done *for them.*

Christ did not commission the Church to be the perpetrators of hatred, death, and carnage. Accusing Christ himself of being anti-Semitic is simply preposterous. He was, in the days of His flesh, a Jew. He was a Jew who spent His life ministering to Jews. His message of love and life was directed to Jews. None need undertake to speak for Him; we need but ponder His own words:

> But I say unto you, Love your enemies, bless them that curse you, do good to them that hate you, and pray for them who despitefully use you, and persecute you (Mt. 5:44).

> O Jerusalem, Jerusalem, which killest the prophets, and stonest them that are sent unto thee, how often would I have gathered thy children together, as a hen doth gather her brood under her wings, and ye would not! (Lk. 13:34).

> Come unto me, all ye that labor and are heavy laden, and I will give you rest. Take my yoke upon you, and learn of me; for I am meek and lowly in heart, and ye shall find rest unto your souls (Mt. 11:28-29).

> Father, forgive them; for they know not what they do (Lk. 23:34).

Some Jewish authorities castigate Jesus for a statement made in John 8:44: "Ye are of your father the devil, and the lusts of your father ye will do." One writer refers to this as one of the two "cardinal themes appearing in Christian anti-Semitism."[1] The conclusion drawn contends that Christ is saying that the Jewish people were children of the devil. This is, in reality, simply not the case. John 8:13 clearly indicates this statement as being made to the Pharisees who were accusing Him of being satanically motivated and indwelt (cp. Jn. 8:48). His accusation is directed toward those religious leaders who had witnessed His miraculous ministry, heard His message, recognized, in truth, what He was doing and saying, then deliberately set about to have Him slain.

His reaction parallels an attitude found in a Jewish woman who had lived through the terrible ordeal experienced by residents of Jerusalem during the darkest hours of the 1948 War of Independence. The city was on the brink of starvation because the Arabs had succeeded in closing the road to Tel Aviv. Heroic Jewish forces, in a desperate effort to save the city and the people, cut a road through the hill country out of reach of the Arab guns. The first convoy reached the city on the Sabbath. She related how she and other weeping Jerusalemites witnessed the arrival of the first trucks, driven by men who were at the point of exhaustion. As the trucks began to rumble into the city, a group of ultra-conservative Jews picked up rocks and began throwing them at the life-bearing convoy. The next day, the same people were in line to receive the supplies brought by the Sabbath-breakers. "Oh, how I hated them!" she explained. Hated whom? The Jewish people? Certainly not. She was proud to be a Jew, and she loved her people dearly. What she rejected was the superficiality and hypocrisy evidenced by a few. To say her statement branded her as a Jew-hater would be as grossly unfair as it is to indict Jesus Christ for His words to the religious leaders of His day who were cut out of the same cloth as their rock-throwing descendants.

The second of the "cardinal themes appearing in Christian anti-Semitism" is drawn from Matthew 27:25: "Then answered all the people, and said, His blood be on us, and on our children." The Jewish commentator states: "The Jews themselves are made to admit their collective responsibility for the crucifixion of the Son of God."[2] In approaching this subject, we must again consider all the Gospel writer actually recorded. Incidentally, he recorded a scene viewed in a historical context. He was an eyewitness. It is presumptuous to claim he inserted the statement with a view toward making life difficult for future generations of Jews. Let us once more examine preceding words: "But the chief priests and elders persuaded the multitude that they should ask for Barabbas, and destroy Jesus" (Mt. 27:20). Matthew declared that the crowd was incited by leaders who had already rejected Christ.

Who Crucified Christ?

In reading the records of the trial and crucifixion objectively, one reaches a rather obvious conclusion, for we see two great representative forces involved in the events which transpired. Jewry, unquestionably, is representative of the religious world. They were the recipients of all of the revealed Word of God. The great divine promises had been committed to them. They were specifically charged with communicating Jehovah's message to the nations of the world. Within the care of this nation rested *truth*. Rome, on the other hand, must stand as the representative of the legal and political world. Thus, the one who served on behalf of the emperor was charged with the responsibility of dispensing the vaunted Roman *justice*. Frail humanity, one segment pledged to truth and the other to justice, was on hand that day. Yet both are guilty of a breach of trust unparalleled in human history. Jewish leaders brought trumped-up charges, suborned witnesses, were guilty of bribery and inciting simple citizens to cry for His blood. A Roman governor examined the charges, declared them to be without foundation, pronounced Him innocent, washed his hands publicly in order to visualize it, then turned Him over to be scourged, humiliated, and crucified. To contend that the Gospel writers soft-peddled Pilate's role in the affair is totally without justification. His part in the travesty is fully magnified. He was not a witless simpleton; he was the emissary of imperial Rome. His saying, in effect, *In the name of Rome, I find him innocent; take him away and crucify him,* demonstrates fully his culpability.

Roman hands fashioned His cross; Jewish voices taunted Him along the way. Roman spikes were battered through His hands and feet; Jewish lips murmured, "So be it." A Roman spear was thrust into His side; a Jew cried, "He saved others; himself he cannot save" (Mt. 27:42; Mk. 15:31). Of Jew and Roman alike it is written, "And sitting down they watched him there" (Mt. 27:36).

The inescapable conclusion is that Jew and Gentile together laid hands on Jesus Christ. It was a crime of humanity. As mankind collectively raised hands against Him, we must join hands in acknowledgment that Jew and Gentile, through their responsible representatives, were joint participants in the loathsome deed. In fact, Gentiles were no less guilty than was the leadership of Israel. To attempt to ascribe primary responsibility to one group or the other is a blatant exercise in hypocrisy.

Some react to what they purport to be harsh phraseology by Christ regarding the future of the Jewish nation. They recoil at His statements of destruction, captivities, and suffering. We might well consider two factors:

1. The pronouncements of Christ are no more severe than those of the prophets of Israel. It is a matter of record that His statements are in complete harmony with those of the prophets.

2. The utterances of Christ, no matter how one may choose to view them, have been realized. What He predicted has taken place

in minute detail. It is inconceivable that any human being could make statements with such telling, long-range accuracy as did Jesus Christ, without His being who He claimed to be.

Neither must we forget that while He proclaimed future suffering, He also unveiled promises of coming glory to as certainly follow. He who revealed the dispersion also announced the return and subsequent establishment of the messianic kingdom when David's greater Son shall reign, "Where'er the sun does its successive journeys run."

EVANGELICAL CHRISTIANS AND THE JEW

A very clear distinction must be drawn between evangelical Christianity and the "Christian" manifestations we have considered. Mr. Will H. Houghton, former president of Moody Bible Institute, states the case generally in a few poetic lines penned many years ago.

Say not a Christian e'er would
    persecute a Jew;
A Gentile might, but not a Christian true.
    Pilate and Roman guard that folly tried.
And with that great Jew's death an empire died!

When Christians gather in a cathedral,
    church or hall,
Hearts turn towards One — the name of Jesus call.
    You cannot persecute — whatever else you do —
The race who gave Him — Jesus was a Jew!

As one cannot speak for every individual within any movement on earth, the word *general* is used as identifying the position which is characteristic of evangelicals. Bear the same distinction in mind when we consider areas where

Jews and evangelicals are said to have compatible views. Not all Jewish leaders will agree that they believe what is set forth. It is to be understood that our comparisons are made with respect to the general position held by the more orthodox elements in Jewry.

The Common Ground

Without attempting a detailed exploration of every compatible area, at least four will demonstrate the point graphically.

    1. The authority of Scripture.
    2. The Abrahamic promises.
    3. The coming Messiah.
    4. The future Kingdom.

Evangelicals firmly adhere to the proposition that "All scripture is given by inspiration of God" (2 Tim. 3:16). This, of course, would include the Old Testament record in its entirety. The Bible is, therefore, the only final and reliable source of revelation on which one may place his faith and order his life.

This being accepted, it follows that the promises of God to Abraham are both literal and permanent. In other words, everything Jehovah has promised to the posterity of the original Hebrew will be delivered to them one day. Evangelical biblicists reject the view which proposed that when the Jews spurned the messianic claims of Christ, Jehovah wrote them off forever then took all of the promises to the Chosen People and transferred them to the Church. This form of theological anti-Semitism is totally foreign to the teachings of the New Testament Scriptures, which emphatically affirm Israel's future in the economy of God as fully anticipated and assured. Thus, in reality, evangelical

Christians are as committed to the basic aspirations of Zionism as are the Jews. We make no apology for being identified as Christian Zionists. Zionism, simply defined, is the belief in the right of the Jewish people to have a national home in Israel.

The promise of a future appearance of the divine Messiah is the great sounding bell of all Scriptures in both Testaments. The hope of the world is not another system but a coming Messiah. Increasingly, Jew and Gentile are reaching the conclusion that every new political ideology crafted by mankind is inadequate. One after another, these human mechanisms have proved a failure. We all know why. No matter how noble our aims, we simply cannot find men who are consistently noble individuals. Undeniably, the fact of history leads one back to the Bible. Its message consistently predicts the failure of man's ingenious designs. Following this, the Scripture affirms man's acknowledgment that the only answer is the appearance of One who is qualified to establish a universal rule. A Jewish friend expressed the rising longing of Jew and Gentile recently as we strolled the streets of Jerusalem. He said, "People are looking for a man to come, someone who can take control." This is not an isolated statement these days, it is fast becoming typical. Evangelicals believe He will come, as the Book declares He will.

When He arrives, a kingdom will be established to cover the earth as the waters cover the sea. The capital city from which the Messiah will reign is destined by divine declaration to be Jerusalem. If one believes the Bible to be authoritative, this is undeniable. All nations will then turn their eyes and dispatch ambassadors toward the venerated soil to present their credentials in the Holy City.

Seat of David's hallowed throne,
　　Salem - City of Peace.
Plagued of death by sword and stone
　　Until all wars shall cease.
Long thy sons have wandered far
　　The captive's chain to bear.
Now, back home, the Royal Star
　　They look with pride to wear.
The Prophets warn of coming strife
　　To smite the remnant there,
But over this shine words of life
　　That vanquish brooding care.
For David's greater Son, you see,
　　Will save and rule the nation,
The Holy City then shall be
　　The center of creation.
　　　　　　　　　　　　　E. McQ.

The Friends of Israel

The aforegoing being true, Jews and biblical Christians share a great deal in common. It is equally true that evangelicals, rather than being entrenched enemies of Jewry, are in actuality the best friends the Jewish people and the state of Israel have on earth. It can be said unequivocally, no group of human beings stand more firmly alongside Israelis than do evangelical Christians. This is easily documented historically from both Jewish and Christian sources. For the sake of our present purpose, we consider only Jewish observations.

An Israeli historian goes on record as saying: "Conversely, the role played by the Old Testament in Calvinism led the Puritan sects to identify themselves with the Jews of the Bible and reflected favorably on their attitudes toward contemporary Jewry."[3] These same Puritan sects later carried their views to America, where they became established as the base on which the traditional American treatment of the Jewish people was erected.

More recently Rabbi Meir Kahane, founder of the militant Jewish Defense League and a man who can hardly be accused of being a Christian sympathizer, made this statement in counseling the state of Israel to view evangelical Christianity as a political ally.

> Israel has within the United States a weapon that itself believes in and can convince others that the United States' true interest is total and unconditional backing of the Jewish State...I refer to the tens of fundamentalist and evangelical Christian Protestant sects, whose members number in the millions and whose leaders have national and international influence...These are groups who are totally Bible oriented, who believe that the Bible is the literal word of God and to whom the literal prophecies of a return to Zion by the Jewish people and the setting up a Jewish state are absolute preconditions for the final redemption...The Christian interest is a simple one, the bringing in of God's Kingdom on Earth and that is clearly done by supporting not only the Jewish State unconditionally, but also opposing any retreat by Israel and urging mass Jewish emigration to the Holy land.[4]

Perhaps the most conclusive comment is found in a declaration concerning the Restoration Movement. The people involved in this movement were evangelical Christians who labored for the establishment and recognition of the state of Israel.

It should be noted that the idea of a Jewish return to Palestine had long found strong support among prominent Christians in Western Europe, particularly in England. Eminent men and women lent themselves to what came to be known as the Restoration Movement, which favored the ingathering of Jews to their Homeland on the grounds of Christian doctrine...It is difficult to say to what extent such pro-Zionist sentiments among Christian leaders influenced the Jews, but in all likelihood they helped pave the way for British acceptance of Zionism later on.[5]

Among those identified with this group was Lord Arthur Balfour, who was the architect of the famous Balfour Declaration. This document was the vehicle by which the British officially pledged support for the establishment of a national home for Jewry in Palestine. The declaration was later incorporated into the League of Nations Mandate for Palestine, July 24, 1922, and paved the way for the historic vote of the United Nations General Assembly which reestablished the state of Israel.

Others who were participants in this movement are referred to in answer to the question, What were the motives of the British Government in issuing the Balfour Declaration?

In all likelihood the decisive factor lay in the personal and moral convictions of the British statesmen who had the Declaration adopted. Balfour saw in it an historic act of reparation to the much-wronged Jewish people, and a chance for it to develop its great gifts in its own home. Balfour was known as a man of

philosophical and detached turn of mind;
those close to him found his emotions deeply
engaged on only one issue — Zionism. Others
like Lloyd George and Smuts were steeped
in the Bible, and the concept of the return
of the Jews strongly appealed to their faith
and sense of tradition.[6]

One more name should be mentioned in this section.
General Sir Edmund Allenby was the British commander of
the Egyptian Expeditionary Force in 1917. He was a superb
general. Of much greater significance, however, is the fact
that he was also a devout Christian. To General Allenby fell
the task of delivering Jerusalem from the Turks. At the root
of his strategy lay his reverent regard for the city of David.
He refused to allow his forces to attack or fire on the Old
City. Instead, he circled north in order to isolate his enemies
and force them to capitulate. Following his victory, he declined
to ride a mount over the street where his Lord had carried
His cross. One will do well to make the contrast been Allenby's
conduct and that of the Crusaders. It will provide a vivid
example of the point under discussion.

It must be immediately emphasized that evangelical
Christians do seek to introduce Jewish people to Jesus Christ
as Messiah-Savior. This is, of course, the central issue
between the Jew and Christian believers. We will as quickly
add that these efforts are never with sword, stone, or
dungeon; but ever with love and a true desire to share the
knowledge of One who has imparted to us light, life, and
peace. Certainly there are those within evangelical groups
who may be regarded as crude and tactless in their efforts
to reach Jewish people. The fundamental point to face,
however, is that when all is said and done the messianic
claims of Jesus Christ must be honestly and intelligently
faced. His credentials, impact on history, and unprecedented
power to transform lives cannot be lightly brushed aside.

General Edmund Allenby enters Jewish Jerusalem, 1917
Courtesy Central Zionist Archives

General Allenby with Jewish community, Chaim Weizmann at his right.
Courtesy Central Zionist Archives

David Lloyd George,
British Prime Minister
Courtesy Central Zionist Archives

Lord Arthur James Balfour,
Author of the Balfour Declaration
Courtesy Central Zionist Archives

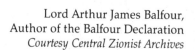

RESTORATION

Israeli paratroopers at the Wailing Wall, 1967
Photograph by David Rubinger
Courtesy Israeli Embassy

If you will it, it is no dream.
Theodor Herzl

CHAPTER FIVE

BACK FROM THE DEAD

FRESH WINDS BLOWING

AN ISRAELI IMMIGRANT stood on a small hill near his kibbutz home. Beside him was a friend from abroad who had come to Israel for a brief visit. Their eyes swept the barren country being developed by the kibbutzniks. "What possessed you to leave the good life in America for these rock-strewn fields?" queried the visitor.

The Israeli thought for a moment then tapped the center of his chest with a forefinger. "Something in here said, 'Go home!' "

That "something in here" was not a new or passing phenomenon in the Jewish anatomy. As long as there has been an Israel, the heart roots of Jewry have been imbedded in the soil just to the south of snow-capped Mount Hermon. While it is historically true that significant portions of the Jewish population have spent varying lengths of time out of the land, it is equally true that the land has never, at any time, been out of the heart of the Jew. Ancient exiles gave voice to it as they sat on the banks of the river Chebar in far off Babylonia.

> By the rivers of Babylon, there we sat down,
> yea, we wept, when we remembered Zion. We
> hung our harps upon the willows in the midst
> thereof. For there they that carried us away
> captive required of us a song; and they that
> wasted us required of us mirth, saying, Sing
> us one of the songs of Zion. How shall we
> sing the LORD's song in a foreign land? If I
> forget thee, O Jerusalem, let my right hand
> forget her cunning. If I do not remember thee,
> let my tongue cleave to the roof of my mouth,
> if I prefer not Jerusalem above my chief joy
> (Ps. 137:1-6).

Later generations, over the protracted exile of the most recent dispersion, would hear Jewish fathers intone during the solemn Passover observance: "Maybe next year in Jerusalem!"

This undying hope is memorialized today each time Israelis raise their voices to sing the national anthem.

> So long as still within our breasts
> The Jewish heart beats true,
> So long as still towards the east
> To Zion looks the Jew.
> So long our hopes are not yet lost —
> Two thousand years we cherished them —
> To live in freedom in the land of
> Zion and Jerusalem.

One writer expresses it this way: "Upheld and fortified in dispersion by the Messianic vision of an ultimate return, the Jews never forgot or forsook their ties with the Homeland. This imperishable hope of redemption gave them fortitude to endure discrimination and persecution...."[1]

For the majority of Jews, until the late 1800's a return to Palestine remained nothing more than a fond hope. But now a freshening breeze began to rise. It was blowing toward the land. With it rose a strange, prompting urgency in the midst of the Jewish people. Something was indeed saying, "The time has come. Let's go home."

To Bible believers, Jew and Gentile, there was never any substantial doubt about this finally coming to pass; never an *if*, only a *when*. The weeping prophet, Jeremiah, saw it, and wrote through his tears.

> Therefore, behold the days come, saith the LORD, that it shall no more be said, The LORD liveth, who brought up the children of Israel out of the land of Egypt, But, The LORD liveth, who brought up the children of Israel from the land of the north, and from all the lands where he had driven them; and I will bring them again into their land that I gave unto their fathers. Behold, I will send for many fishers, saith the LORD, and they shall fish them; and afterward will I send for many hunters, and they shall hunt them from every mountain, and from every hill, and out of the clefts of the rocks (Jer. 16:14-16).

Of course, the full weight of the prophet's words will be experienced during the age of the messianic reign. However, one would find it difficult to deny that the initial sickle thrusts of the final harvest-home movement were made about the turn of the century.

Theodor Herzl was among the first to interpret and assimilate the quickening breeze of the impending Jewish return. Herzl, a journalist from Vienna, had for some time entertained doubts about the quality of hospitality Jewish people were receiving from their Gentile host nations. His suspicions were confirmed as he witnessed the humiliation of Alfred Dreyfus in Paris in 1894. Dreyfus, choosing a career in the military, had risen to the rank of captain and was appointed to the general staff of the French army — the only Jew to serve in this position. He later was accused of treason and tried before a court martial. After two trials and years in prison, he was exonerated of all charges placed against him. However, the anti-Semitic furor which was fanned by the trial shocked Herzl and European Jewry. It was during this time that Herzl became convinced that the future of the Jews of Europe was very dark.

There is one interesting sidelight which we should examine in passing. The Scriptures declare the fact that even the wrath of the most ungodly of men is often turned toward accomplishing divine purposes. A case in point is Karl Lueger, who served as the mayor of Vienna in the 1890's. He was openly anti-Jewish and made his views a part of his political platform. Adolf Hitler was enraptured by Lueger's anti-Semitic oratorical outbursts when he came to Vienna to study. It was this same Karl Lueger who was in the mind of Herzl as he watched the degradation of Alfred Dreyfus in Paris. He concluded that if anti-Semitism could successfully prevail in the two most enlightened cities in Europe, it could no longer be viewed as a temporary manifestation. While Lueger willingly made his contribution to the impending Holocaust, he unwittingly helped set the stage for the reestablishment of the state of Israel.

First Zionist Congress

It must have seemed strange to the people of Basle, Switzerland to see Jews in frock coats and white ties moving through the streets to attend the opening session of the

David Ben Gurion,
First Prime Minister of Israel
Courtesy Central Zionist Archives

Theodor Herzl,
Founder of the modern state of Israel
Courtesy Central Zionist Archives

First Zionist Congress. Herzl had insisted that the attire of delegates befit the appearance of officials of state. Most of the world did not give passing notice to this first assembly of Jews with a dream. Indeed, even among Jews, the gathering was not only ignored by many but engendered outright opposition from others. Among Herzl's own friends were those who confided that he had gone quite mad. They went so far as to frankly counsel him to see a psychiatrist. Frontal opposition came from rabbinical forces in Germany, who officially advised Jews to shun Zionism.

Herzl and his like-minded contemporaries were not deterred. To him the only long-term option realistically open was an autonomous state for Jews. His belief in the solemn significance of the initial assembly of Jewish representatives was recorded in his diary at the close of the historic gathering: "At Basle I founded the Jewish state."[2]

Max Nordau drafted a document which set forth Zionist aims. The opening statement is a concise summary of what Zionism involves. "Zionism seeks to establish a home for the Jewish people in Palestine secured under public law."[3]

By the time the last session drew to a close, Zionists had created a political forum, an official press, and a bank. The dream nation also had an ensign. "It is with a flag that people are led to wherever one desires, even to the Promised Land."[4] The now-familiar design incorporated two blue stripes and the star of David on a white field.

Which Way Home?

Jews would go home; the question was, Where would home be? As surprising as this might seem, it was a serious consideration. Early efforts to deal with the Ottoman Turks, who were in control of Palestine at this time, proved futile. They would not agree to an independent Jewish state in the area. North America and Argentina were suggested as alternatives. African Uganda was offered by the British. A special commission was dispatched to explore the feasibility of the proposal. Ultimately, the Uganda scheme was rejected. Cyprus and El Arish, in the Sinai Peninsula, were also viewed as prospective areas for settlement. It was not to be. The Jewish people had a homeland: Eretz Israel. The divine magnetism of the Land would prove irresistible. "And the LORD thy God will bring thee into the land which thy fathers possessed, and thou shalt possess it" (Dt. 30:5).

The Ascenders

While the official struggle for political status in Palestine continued, "Practical Zionists" proceeded on the assumption that their rights in Israel were self-evident. They would win the land with "Another cow, another dunam" (one-quarter acre of land).

These early waves of immigrants were known as *Aliyah* (Ascenders). The impetus for their desire to enter the land was the savage series of Pogroms being carried out in Russia. By 1903, the close of the period of the First Aliyah, 90,000 acres of land had been purchased and approximately 10,000 new Jewish settlers had entered Israel. The Second Aliyah (1904-1914) brought some 40,000 new immigrants. By 1914 the Jewish population in Israel had swelled to 85,000.

The tactic was simple. Settlers would buy up land wherever it was made available. Financing for these lands was provided by foreign patrons — most notably Baron Edmond James de Rothschild. Settlements were established, and Jews began to develop the newly acquired properties. Most of the land made available was considered worthless by the former owners — wasteland and malaria-infested swamps. These swamps would soon be drained to one day produce the verdant farms now occupying the countryside around the

Sea of Galilee. It was in this period that the famous kibbutz concept was implemented.

It was a beginning. Generations of Jewish people had gone to their graves with an unrealized hope of witnessing this new day. Others had despaired and forfeited any belief it could ever become a reality. But Jews were now, in fact, back in the land in significant numbers. The same weighty hand of persecution which had driven them out now appeared to be inexorably driving them back.

As immigrants to Palestine went about the work of reviving the land and world Jewry observed with growing fascination, clouds began to gather over the world. Two wars, global in scope, were approaching. Between them lay a time of prosperity, followed by a crushing depression which destroyed financial empires and imposed crippling poverty on the industrialized nations. These tumultuous years would see the face of the map of Europe altered and new political forces set in motion. Prophetically, the pace was to quicken with events long anticipated by earnest watchers dramatically seizing the attention of the international community.

THREE MINUTES TO RESURRECTION

"The voting itself took only three minutes, but it seemed to stretch the length of the exile." Dov Joseph, military governor of Jerusalem during the War of Independence, was summing up his emotions during the climactic vote of the Security Council of the United Nations in November, 1947. His words could well represent the feelings of the majority of Jewry the world over.

The journey had been long and arduous; but the miracle nation had now arrived at a point unparalleled in the history of humanity. It would be a one-of-a-kind phenomenon. Israel would wear the crowning distinction of being the only ancient nation ever to be resurrected and restored as a national entity.

Immigrants camp near Haifa, 1920
Courtesy Central Zionist Archives

Kibbutz laborers, Ein Harod, 1926
Courtesy Central Zionist Archives

A companion manifestation would be the resuscitation, again for the first time, of an ancient language — Hebrew. If one of the ancients were to stroll through Zion Square in Jerusalem today, the words passing the lips of young Sabras and elderly immigrants would quickly assure him of being home and among his own.

Dov Joseph's backward glance during those unprecedented moments in 1947 could have paused fleetingly at several milestones which were woven into the fabric of the restoration of the nation.

The Balfour Declaration

The first long step in the establishment of modern Israel was taken when the British government officially recognized Zionist aspirations and gave voice to their support in the Balfour Declaration, November 2, 1917. The declaration itself was named for Arthur James Balfour, who was one of the initial advocates of a national home for Jewry. At this time he served Britain as foreign secretary. Other prominent names associated with the document were Lloyd George, the prime minister, and Chaim Weizmann, later to become the first president of the fledgling state.

The declaration itself amounted to a statement of sympathy with Zionist goals. Balfour communicated the text of the decision to Lord Rothschild in a letter dated November 2, 1917.

> Dear Lord Rothschild,
>
> I have much pleasure in conveying to you, on behalf of His Majesty's Government, the following declaration of sympathy with the Jewish Zionist aspirations which have been submitted to, and approved by, the Cabinet.
>
> "His Majesty's Government view with favour the establishment in Palestine of a

national home for the Jewish people, and will use their best endeavours to facilitate the achievement of this object, it being clearly understood that nothing shall be done which may prejudice the civil and religious rights of existing non-Jewish communities in Palestine, or the rights and political status enjoyed by Jews in any other country."

I should be grateful if you would bring this declaration to the knowledge of the Zionist Federation.

Yours sincerely,
Arthur James Balfour

From the practical side, several elements were bound up in the human aspects of the declaration. Field Marshall Smuts, a member of the British war cabinet, summarized these motivating factors in a speech given in London in 1919. "It would rally Jewry on a world-wide scale to the Allied cause."[5] He further listed moral and religious factors as major considerations — we have already mentioned the biblical views held by Balfour. An additional point of leverage was the personal contribution made by Dr. Chaim Weizmann to the British war effort. Dr. Weizmann was a chemist and aided materially in the development of military weapons.

Arab leaders were favorably disposed to the idea of a Jewish state at this time. King Hussein wrote:

We saw the Jews...streaming to Palestine from Russia, Germany, Austria, Spain, America...The cause of causes could not escape those who had the gift of deeper insight; they know that the country was for its original sons, for all their differences, a sacred and beloved homeland.[6]

In January of 1919 King Hussein's son, Emir Feisal, chief Arab delegate to the Paris Peace Conference, and Dr. Weizmann concluded an agreement endorsing the Balfour Declaration. Arab recognition and diplomatic relations were pledges, conditioned by French consideration of Arab interests in other territories.

As Baron Rothschild scanned the historic document, he must have been taken with a sense of standing in the full flow of onrushing history. Balfour's note was the harbinger of larger events which loomed on the horizon.

World War I

For 400 years (1516-1917) the Ottoman Turks were caretakers of the land. Before them a succession of would-be sovereigns had aspired to permanently possess Palestine. The Roman occupation endured from 63 B.C. through 395 A.D. They were supplanted by the Byzantines who stayed until the Arabs deposed them in 636. The Arabs were set upon and put to flight by the Seljuks in 1099, only to be chased themselves by menacing Mamlukes in 1291. The Mamlukes would fare no better than their predecessors. They fell prey to the Ottoman Turks in 1516. Doggedly they came, seeking to possess the land of Abraham. As certainly as they entered, they would be spewed out.

> Long they looked with hungry eyes
>   At Canaan's storied land,
> Stealthily conspired to come
>   And take the deed in hand.
>
> Columned armies, turbaned hosts,
>   Dark Bedouin marauder,
> Swept with fury o'er the hills
>   To seize Jehovah's daughter.

> With dented shield and blunted sword
>   They all would trudge away,
> And learn that only Jacob's sons
>   Could enter there to stay.
>   E. McQ.

While this game of imperial musical chairs was going on, the divine program for Israel was slowly unfolding. Events were in process which would order circumstances and create the opportunity for Jews to return home.

Four hundred and one years after the oppressive Ottoman reign began, Sir Edmund Allenby stood viewing the walled city of Jerusalem. His expeditionary force had successfully rolled through Beersheba, Gaza, and Jaffa. Now he was about to possess the pearl — Jerusalem. On December 11, 1917 General Allenby, as the official emissary of the British crown, strode through the streets of the Old City in ceremonial gesture marking the end of Ottoman rule.

The British Mandate

The ouster of the Turks ushered in a period which would see the foundations laid for the reestablishment of Israel. The Mandate for Palestine (July 24, 1922) called for British oversight of the area. Incorporated into the Mandate was the Balfour Declaration recognizing the rights of Jews to establish a state.

The next 30 years of British rule were characterized by accelerated differences and growing tension. This condition would ultimately mature into open hostility which would predicate British withdrawal in May of 1948.

Originally, the Mandate extended over both sides of the Jordan; but in 1922 the British divided the territory into two sections, thus creating the Arab emirate of Jordan.

British policy on immigration fluctuated during these years. At times Jews were allowed to come. Periodically, however, they would be severely restricted in the number allowed to enter. Also forbidden was the purchase of land. The final straw fell with the announcement of the White Paper of 1939. Under its provisions, Jews entering Israel would be limited to 75,000 over the next five years. At that time immigration would be closed to Jews. During these years European Jewry would face the most traumatic tidal wave of terror ever inflicted upon them — the Nazi Holocaust. To close the door of the homeland to the waves of refugees was, in the eyes of the Jews, insufferable.

By now major portions of the decimated nation in exile were fully convinced of the necessity of having a place to go. The inner urge had turned into a settled conviction which could no longer be denied. Jews would go home; they would have it no other way.

A Nation Reborn

The postwar world reeled under the impact of the full disclosure of the indescribable horrors of the Holocaust. That 6,000,000 Jews could be systematically exterminated in a country which boasted intellectual and theological enlightenment cast a pall of stunned silence over a war-weary planet.

The world had become aware of the extent of the Nazi atrocities in the summer of 1943. As a result, the British government, the United States, and the Jewish Haganah undertook efforts to facilitate the flight of Jewish refugees. Approximately 41,000 Jews reached Palestine between 1943 and 1945.

At war's end the British again pursued a repressive course toward immigrants attempting to leave the horrors of Europe far behind them. Ships carrying refugees were impounded

The *Exodus* with illegal immigrants in Haifa harbor, 1947
Courtesy Central Zionist Archives

Shabbelai Lozinski, aground near Haifa, 1947
Courtesy Central Zionist Archives

or turned back to their points of embarkation. Many Jews were placed in internment camps and detained indefinitely. Still they persisted in their attempts to get back to the land. Between 1945 and 1948 65 immigrant ships embarked for Palestine. Some were intercepted before they could deliver their human cargo. Others were purposely run aground and the passengers unceremoniously discharged. At Ashdod, in 1947, a vessel named the *Shabbelai Lozinski* went aground. As British officials began to converge on the scene, local residents rushed to the water's edge and quickly began to mingle with the incoming strangers. By the time the British arrived, it was impossible for them to distinguish between immigrant and resident.

The climactic incident arose when the *Exodus,* with 4,515 refugees on board, arrived off the coast of Palestine in 1947. When the British boarded the ship, an altercation broke out between members of the crew and the boarding party. The melee left three dead and 28 injured. All passengers were quickly transferred to three other vessels and transported to France. Upon their arrival, French officials found shiploads of Jews who adamantly refused to disembark. They had boarded the *Exodus* with intentions to go to Israel, and Israel it would be. The French conferred and decided not to remove them against their collective will. The ships moved on to Hamburg, Germany, where authorities were less disposed to consider the desires of the passengers. They were forcibly evicted from the ships and moved to an internment camp inside Germany. The event served to arouse international opinion against British immigration policy.

Inside Israel, Jews were mounting organized opposition to continued British domination. British policy now clearly favored Arab interests. Consequently, they were caught in the jaws of both Jew and Arab. Jews were becoming increasingly militant; Arabs became ever more demanding.

Jewish residents settled on two firm objectives: force an end to the Mandate; open the shores of the Mediterranean to Jewish refugees. Resistance organizations began to harass the British. Haganah followed the directive of official Jewish bodies. Other groups, most notably Lehi and Irgun, acted independently. By 1947 the sorely tried British were ready to turn the entire matter over to the United Nations for a solution.

The U.N. commissioned representatives of 11 member states as a United Nations Special Committee on Palestine. Their recommendation would partition Palestine into independent Jewish and Arab states. These states were to share economic union. Jerusalem was to be placed under international control.

On November 29, 1947, the delegates of the United Nations General Assembly gathered at Flushing Meadow, New York, to consider the committee's recommendation. The dramatic roll call recorded 33 in favor, 13 opposed and 10 abstentions — *Israel was reborn!*

The response was immediate and global. Jews danced in the streets, wept in their synagogues, and erected grand dreams for the future. Universally they joined hands with Jews of a long-gone day.

> When the LORD turned again the captivity of Zion, we were like them that dream. Then was our mouth filled with laughter, and our tongue with singing; then said they among the nations, The LORD hath done great things for them. The LORD hath done great things for us, whereof we are glad (Ps. 126:1-3).

Jewry was seized with the euphoric realization that it would be this generation which would touch ground on the majestic prophetic pinnacle. It would be for them and their children to sing of former dreams, "Two thousand years we cherished them — to live in freedom in the land of Zion and Jerusalem." It was no longer the stuff of dreams; it was historical fact!

War of Independence

The U.N. decision was just that, a decision. At this point Israel was a paper nation. The Mandate would continue in force for another six months. British forces were to be withdrawn on May 5, 1948.

The Arabs rejected the Partition Plan and immediately began violent operations against the Jews. Strikes, riots, and armed attacks were all involved in their strategy. While the Arabs were restrained from launching all-out military efforts by the presence of the British, they initiated a series of localized assaults. The British were indifferent to these activities. As a matter of fact, during the months of hasty preparation for the impending war (November-May), the English rigidly enforced strictures against the Jews importing arms. Arabs, however, were allowed to mobilize for the conflict to come.

As the day of the British withdrawal drew near, many who had supported the resolution in the U.N. began to waver. It appeared that the handwriting was on the wall. Israel could not be expected to hold out against the superior numbers and better equipment of the Arabs. On March 19th, the United States withdrew its endorsement of the plan. General George Marshall, Secretary of State, counseled his friend David Ben-Gurion to bide his time until a more favorable political climate could develop. Perhaps, the general thought, arrangements could be made whereby the United Nations could play an active role in implementing the plan.

Ben-Gurion reflected on his thoughts during these days:

> Here, then, was the counsel of a friend and
> the military appreciation of our situation by
> one of the world's outstanding soldiers. On
> the face of it, such advice could not be
> dismissed lightly. Yet it could not deflect us
> from our chosen course. For Marshall could
> not know what we knew — what we felt in
> our very bones: that this was our historic hour;
> if we did not live up to it, through fear or
> weakness of spirit, it might be generations or
> even centuries before our people were given
> another historic opportunity — if indeed we
> would be alive as a national group.[7]

General Marshall suggested that the U.N. establish a trusteeship over Palestine which would continue in force until a suitable agreement could be reached. This proposal was categorically rejected. There could be no turning back now. Israel would face whatever prospects lay in store for her.

On May 14, 1948 the National Council, which was destined to become the provisional government for the new state, adopted a Declaration of the Establishment of the Jewish State. This Declaration of Independence closed with a plea:

> We appeal to the Jewish people throughout
> the Diaspora to rally round the Jews of Eretz
> Israel in the tasks of immigration and upbuild-
> ing and to stand by them in the great struggle
> for the realization of the age-old dream — the
> redemption of Israel.[8]

After the signing ceremony by the members of the council, David Ben-Gurion rose to his feet to announce, "The state of Israel has risen!"

Sir Alan Cunningham, the last British High Commissioner, boarded a destroyer in Haifa harbor at midnight. The next day, May 15th, British forces withdrew. The Mandate was officially over. With its demise the stage was set for the nation's struggle for survival.

The Fighting

Battles would be fought intermittently over the next 13 months. Immediately following the British withdrawal, Arab armies rolled into the country. Egyptians, Syrians, Iraqis, the Transjordanian Arab Legion, and the Liberation Army all hastened to accomplish Israel's being stillborn.

For a month the contest raged up and down the land. Hard pressed Jewish forces, initially without a tank, fighter plane, or field gun, suffered heavy casualties. The Haganah fought desperately to maintain a corridor from the coast to Jerusalem. This proved to be a formidable task, which the Arabs finally succeeded in making impossible. Jerusalem was besieged.

Inside the Old City, the Jewish Quarter came under heavy attack by contingents of the Elite Arab Legion. Jewish resistance was no less than heroic. The area was defended street by street and building by building. At one point, Palmach forces managed to penetrate through the Zion Gate and made contact with the Jewish defenders. The advantage could not be maintained, however, and the quarter was surrendered on May 25th. Jews were expelled from their homes and places of worship. It would be nearly 20 years before they could return.

Elsewhere, military supplies were coming into the country in a comparative trickle, and prospects of the Arabs accomplishing their purpose began to look promising for them.

During this time the U.N. Security Council was calling for a cease-fire. Israel was agreeable, but the Arabs were reluctant to accept the proposal. Finally, they relented and a truce was called. It went into effect on June 11th.

The truce expired on July 9, 1948, and fighting resumed. With the resumption of hostilities, the Arabs discovered a drastic turn of events. During the period of the truce, the Jews had managed some incredible feats in securing and transporting vital military supplies into Israel. It was now the Arabs who were to feel the lash. The Egyptians were first in line. The day before the expiration of the truce, July 8th, Egyptian troops renewed attacks in the south. Their goal was to cut off the Negev. Israelis were prepared. Strong fortifications and mobile commandoes, dubbed "Samson's Foxes," met the attackers head-on. Within ten days the dazed Egyptians would find their assault shattered, casualties high, and much of their equipment in Jewish hands.

The ten days' fighting would find Arabs falling to the same fate in other sectors as well. Israeli troops took Ramleh, Lydda, and Nazareth. The main body of the Liberation Army was driven back into Lebanon. In the air, Jewish bombers began making runs over Cairo and Damascus.

A new cease-fire was proposed. The Arabs now had ready ears; the Jews were the reluctant party. The new truce went into effect on July 17 in Jerusalem and the next day in the rest of the country.

Fighting would again break out in mid-October. This round saw Jews taking Beersheba and a number of villages on the Lebanese border. Vital roads were secured and new supply routes won. All hostilities were concluded by January 7, 1949. The War of Independence was over.

Israel was now a fact. The price had been high — 4,000 soldiers and 2,000 civilians had forfeited their lives. The financial cost, 500 million dollars, seemed astronomical to the tiny nation with so few resources. But the state was intact. They did not yet possess Old Jerusalem. Other strategic areas remained in Arab hands. Jerusalem was designated as the capital of the nation. Headquarters were opened in the Jewish Agency. Chaim Weizmann spoke at the opening meeting of the Provisional Council of State:

> This is a great day in our lives. Let it not be regarded as undue arrogance if we say that it is also a great day in the life of the world. Tidings of encouragement and hope go forth at this hour from this house, from this Holy city, to all the persecuted and oppressed the world over who strive for liberty and equality. There is recompense for a righteous struggle. If we, the suffering and wretched people, impoverished and downtrodden, have been privileged to celebrate this occasion, there is hope for all those who aspire for justice and righteousness.[9]

The State of Israel will be open to Jewish immigration and the ingathering of exiles. It will devote itself to developing the Land for the good of all its inhabitants.

Israeli Proclamation
of Independence
May 14, 1948

CHAPTER SIX

ON EAGLES' WINGS

"THEN THE LORD THY GOD will turn thy captivity, and have compassion upon thee, and will return and gather thee from all the nations where the LORD thy God hath scattered thee" (Dt. 30:3).

The prophet's words reverberated throughout the nations where Jews were awaiting their summons to return home. From the far corners of the world they began the long trek back to the land. In Jewish terminology, it was the "ingathering of the exiles." Implementation of the prophetic word soon became a national obsession. In 1950 the "Law of the Return" became a legislated reality. It granted every Jew the automatic right to become an *oleh* (immigrant) and make his home in Israel. The Citizenship Law, adopted in 1952, granted every Jewish immigrant instant citizenship the moment his foot touched Israeli soil.

Jeremiah's "hunters" and "fishers" (Jer. 16:16) moved out to ply the highways and sea-lanes in quest of Hebrews to woo homeward. From May 15, 1948 through the close of 1951, 684,201 immigrants had found their way back to Israel. At the peak of the initial wave of immigration, a thousand people a day were streaming through the reception centers. Twenty-five thousand came from the internment camps on Cyprus. Hard on their heels were another 70,000 survivors of the Holocaust from Germany, Italy, and Austria. In the first year following independence, a total of 42 countries contributed Jews to the new-old land. Indeed, the face of the Jewish population centers was experiencing radical changes. In some instances entire communities transferred places of residence. A few countries found the Jewish population almost entirely gone from their midst. Worthy examples of this relocation process are:

> Iraq — 121,512 of 130,000 resident Jews
> Bulgaria — 37,000 of 45,000 population
> Libya — 30,500 of 35,000 Jewish residents
> Poland — 103,723 (two-thirds of all Jews)
> Rumania — 118,940 (one-third of the Jewish people)
> Yemen — All Jews returned

As Doves to Their Windows

Isaiah peered down the long prophetic corridor and inquired:

> Who are these that fly like a cloud, and like the doves to their windows? Surely the coasts shall wait for me, and the ships of Tarshish first, to bring thy sons from far (Isa. 60:8-9).

Although he did not know their precise identity, Isaiah did predict their method of arrival — by sea and air!

The Yemenites and Iraqis provide magnificent illustrations of what the prophet was viewing.

Yemenite Jews had been out of the homeland, it is believed, since the days of Solomon, Israel's third sovereign. Yet, they had never found a permanent home in their *new* land. With the coming of independence, the Yemenites were gripped by a surge of messianic fervor — it was clearly time to return home. Consequently, thousands began making their way south toward the seaports in Aden on foot. They carried with them all of their earthly possessions. Upon learning of the mass migration, Israeli officials began negotiations with Yemen and the British authorities in Aden. An agreement was reached in May of 1949, and *Operation Magic Carpet* began. Israelis watched as an assortment of aircraft swept into the skies and banked in graceful arcs toward the southeast. Their mission: to transport Yemenite Jews "on eagles' wings" (Ex. 19:4) home to Israel. By the time the operation came to a close, some 47,000 Yemenites were returned. Of the total population, no more than a few hundred remained in Yemen. An Israeli authority stated recently that there are no Jews in Yemen today.

"Who are these that fly like a cloud, and like the doves to the windows?" At least 47,000 of them were Yemenite Jews!

One year later, a repeat performance was done, this time with Iraqi Jews. In March of 1950 the Iraqi government announced a "Special Law Authorizing the Emigration of Jews." In order to qualify, Iraqi citizenship was to be renounced. Also, each person would be allowed to take no more than $16.00 out of the country — children were allowed even smaller amounts. All Jews over 20 years of age were eligible. It meant all proceeds from land and personal property sales must be left behind. This time the Jewish Agency decided on a more biblical operation designation. *Operation Ezra and Nehemiah* would guide these home-hungry returnees. Over the next 18 months 121,512 Iraqi Jews were flown to Cyprus, then went on to Israel by sea and air.

"Who are these that fly like a cloud, and like the doves to their windows?" At least 121,512 more were Iraqi Jews.

Immigration

These spectacular events serve as points of emphasis which focus on the importance of immigration to the nation. Israelis view the *olim* (immigrants) as the lifeblood of the state. One of the most obvious current problems faced by Israel is a reduced immigration rate. Worldwide efforts are being made to encourage an increase in the number of returnees.

Thus far there have been four major waves of immigration:

May 1948 through 1951 —
754,800 entered the country, doubling the population.
1955 through 1957 —
Large numbers of Jews from Morocco, Tunisia, Poland, and Rumania provided the core of new arrivals.
1961 through 1964 —
215,056 came from Eastern Europe and North Africa.
After the Six-Day War (1967) —
262,000 arrived, principally from North and South America, Western Europe, and the Soviet Union.

In the early days, the *olim* were housed in comparatively primitive quarters — many lived in tents. Today, they are taken immediately to new homes or absorption centers.

In the years since statehood was gained, Israel has experienced a fivefold increase in population. Between May of 1948 and May of 1973 the population rose from 650,000 to 3,240,400.

All of these newcomers learn Hebrew. This can be accomplished rather quickly by attending an *ulpan* — a special school teaching an intensive, six-month course in the language.

Mass immigration over an extended period does pose some formidable problems. In Israel it is the matter of cultural integration. Bridging this cultural gap is a major thrust of the Ministry of Immigration and Absorption. The scope of this problem may be seen by comparing the extreme differences in cultural backgrounds of Jewish people from Moslem countries, such as North Africa and Asia, and those from America and Europe. One will observe vast differences in social, political, and technological concepts. The problem of full assimilation of immigrants into Israeli life is repeatedly named as one of the greatest contemporary challenges faced today.

Opinions vary as to how satisfactory integration can best be accomplished. All agree that the first step in achieving unification is the mastery of Hebrew. The next is logically seen in the field of education. Students from underdeveloped countries are provided special opportunities designed to move them toward equality with their more advantaged kinsmen. Israelis look confidently toward a final solution to this dilemma.

At this writing, Jews born in Israel exceed the number of immigrants entering the country by approximately one-half — 629,500 to 315,000 between 1967 and 1972.

The Land

Travelers to Palestine in the 19th and 20th centuries were struck by the barrenness of the land. Most saw little to be desired apart from the historical attachment to religious holy places. It was an area which caused these self-same travelers to pose a question that had been anticipated long before by Moses:

> ...the foreigner who shall come from a far land, shall say, when they see the plagues of that land...that it is not sown, nor beareth, nor any grass groweth therein...Wherefore hath the LORD done thus unto this land? (Dt. 29:22-24).

New immigrants learn Hebrew at Ulpan in upper Nazareth
Courtesy Israeli Embassy

Yemenite Jews arriving in Israel
Courtesy Central Zionist Archives

Golda Meir dedicating a forest on Mount Gilboa, 1947
Courtesy Central Zionist Archives

The American writer, Mark Twain, declared, "Over it broods the spell of a curse that has withered its fields and fettered its energies...desolate and unlovely."[1]

Alphonse de Lamartine referred to its barrenness as "...The tomb of a whole people."[2]

One can well understand why they were inclined to make such statements. For centuries the land had been afflicted by calculated destructiveness. A succession of armies had warmed themselves by fires built from the woodlands of Israel. Finally, the hills would stand denuded with no more fuel to offer imperial encampments. Animals of wandering Bedouins foraged among the same hills for what sparse greenery remained. Attempts at agricultural pursuits were a thing of the past. As foreigners raised their questions about the underlying causes of this condition, a wasted land awaited the return of her native sons.

Mark Twain and his querying fellow travelers would most certainly have lifted skeptical brows at the prophet's confident prediction:

> The wilderness and the solitary place shall be glad for them; and the desert shall rejoice, and blossom like the rose. It shall blossom abundantly, and rejoice even with joy and singing; the glory of Lebanon shall be given unto it, the excellency of Carmel and Sharon; they shall see the glory of the LORD, and the excellency of our God (Isa. 35:1-2).

Let it be said of these words that in the terms of primary reference, they apply to the glory of the coming Millennial Age. However, we must also be aware of our privilege at being allowed a preview of coming events. If the transformation which has taken place in Israel is only the bud, what must the full flower of fulfillment hold in store?

It is doubtful that any nation in history has taken such long steps in so short a time as has Israel. Malaria-infested swamps and arid desert regions have undergone astounding changes. Our aforementioned travelers, could they make a return visit, would be hard put to believe they were in the same land. Northern valleys are carpeted with green. Hillsides abound with maturing forests. Jerusalem pine, tamarisk, eucalyptus, and acacia now thrust skyward on hills down the length of the country. To the south, desert lands stand deep in ripening grain. The Jordan Valley yields abundant harvests of succulent produce. Dates, bananas, avocados, and mangoes are among produce items grown here and along the coastal plain. Coastal areas and the hill country are dotted by emerald citrus groves.

Tobacco, cotton, sugar beets, groundnuts, and vegetables of all varieties spring from the soil, while hothouses grow millions of blooms for export and domestic use. Roses, gladioli, tulips, and chrysanthemums are familiar names among floral producers.

From Dan to Beersheba, from the Jordan to the sea, the land has taken on a new look.

Before statehood was achieved, 11,120 acres had been reclaimed. Between 1948 and 1971 this total escalated to 119,293 acres in the hill country and Negev. Another 110,456 acres were claimed through the drainage of swamplands.

Much of the recovered area is watered by means of irrigation. Water sources come almost exclusively from the Jordan River and the Sea of Galilee. Maintaining an adequate water supply is a constant source of vexation for Israeli agricultural planners. The northern region benefits from sufficient rainfall. In the near desert areas to the south, however, rain is a very scarce commodity. In order to distribute available water supplies, Israel has developed a national plan for irrigation. Under this program, 90 percent of accessible water is used to irrigate lands totaling in excess of 453,700 acres.

To accomplish this, a prodigious project, The National Water Carrier, was undertaken. This carrier provides a central artery through which water is pumped from the Sea of Galilee then transported by canal and tunnel, pulled mainly by gravitational force, all the way down to waiting fields in the Negev.

The problem of providing additional water for irrigation is a priority matter for Israeli technologists and scientists. The most promising answer rests with the development of satisfactory methods of desalinating vast quantities of sea water. One such project is already in operation at Eilat. Another larger facility is under construction at Ashdod. Nuclear powered dual-purpose plants, which will not only desalinate sea water but also serve as electric power sources, are now under study.

Nearly 500 new villages and settlements were established between 1948 and 1972. These dot the face of the land alongside those built before and since. They are in the main agricultural settlements — although some now also contain industrial facilities. Westerners are familiar with the kibbutz, a collective communal settlement in which property is owned by the commune. Less familiar, but much more popular these days, is the moshav. Under this arrangement, each family owns and manages its own farm. The cooperative principle is retained, with produce being sold and equipment purchased through a central cooperative agency. There are now nearly 400 moshavim operating in Israel. The vast majority of new settlements now being established use this system.

Israel now produces enough fruit, vegetables, poultry, eggs, milk, and dairy products to meet all national demands and supply foodstuffs for export as well. A variety of grains must still be imported in significant quantities; but even in this area, Israelis satisfy approximately one-half of the national demand.

Industry

Industrial growth has kept pace with other segments of national development. The textile industry supplies about one-quarter of industrial exports. An electronics products industry is experiencing rapid growth. Israel is currently vying with Belgium for the exclusive position of being the diamond center of the world. Her diamond merchants hold a near monopoly on the medium-sized stones which are an Israeli specialty. Israel Aircraft Industry Ltd. is the country's largest industrial enterprise. Among its products are the Arava passenger cargo plane, the Fouga Magister jet trainer, and an executive aircraft, The Westwind.

Other industrial branches which the government is encouraging and assisting are furs, clothing, leather goods, agricultural implements, machinery, die casting, and medical equipment.

Between 1950 and 1972 industrial production in Israel increased by an average of ten percent a year. Industrial exports grew at an average rate of 20 percent per annum during this same period.

Minerals

Israelis often lament their lack of large quantities of oil. Although there is some oil and gas production in the country, it is extremely meager when compared with some of their Middle Eastern neighbors. While this may be true regarding oil resources, in mineral wealth Israel cannot be named among the pauper nations.

Deuteronomy 8:9 calls Palestine "a land whose stones are iron, and out of whose hills thou mayest dig bronze." The Timna copper deposits have born out the accuracy of the Mosaic statement. The Timna mines are located in a region about 15 miles north of Eilat. Nearby are the remains of the mines of King Solomon and another era. Ore reserves here are estimated to total 20 million tons. Both surface and underground methods are employed to extract the ore.

Geological surveys have revealed that much of the nation's mineral wealth rests beneath the sands of the Negev. Large deposits of phosphates have been discovered there. Israel's phosphorite is used mainly for producing fertilizer.

Building products are produced from an enormous stone supply suitable for quarrying and crushing. Limestone is used for commercial marble and building. Cement is another essential product which is available in abundance. Gypsum is quarried and shipped in from an area near the Gulf of Suez.

The greatest concentration of mineral wealth is found in the Dead Sea. This body of water is unique in that it has an inlet but no provision for egress. For thousands of years the Jordan has emptied its flow into the Dead Sea. High year-round temperatures cause the concentration and deposit of huge quantities of mineral substances. What it amounts to, actually, is a vast natural mining system which, over the centuries, has stored enticing reserves against the day when Jacob's sons would return to recover it.

In total area, the Dead Sea covers 393 square miles. It is the most saline of all the world's bodies of water. The average salt concentration stands between 28 and 31 percent. The Dead Sea is known to contain billions of tons of magnesium chloride, common salt, potassium chloride, magnesium bromide, and calcium chloride.

Tomatoes grow in the Negev
Courtesy Israeli Embassy

Potash Works at Sodom on the Dead Sea
Courtesy Israeli Embassy

Theodor Herzl was fully aware of the strategic value of the Dead Sea and wrote of its importance in 1902. He specifically mentioned potassium, bromide, and magnesium and saw great promise for future extraction of these minerals.

To Take a Spoil

Israel's vast reserves of mineral resources prove to be one of the prime inducements encouraging the end-time intrusions into the Middle East predicted by the Jewish prophets. Perhaps the most graphic description of one of these invasions is found in the writings of Ezekiel, as he outlines events which will take place in "the latter years." The striking revelation clearly identifies the motivation for this aggressive excursion into the land of milk and honey. Ezekiel's confident prediction recorded the thoughts of the invaders well over 2,000 years before it occured to them!

> After many days thou shalt be visited; *in the latter years thou shalt come into the land* that is brought back from the sword, and is gathered out of many peoples, against the mountains of Israel, which have been always waste; but it is brought forth out of the nations, and they shall dwell safely, all of them...And thou shalt say, I will go up to the land of unwalled villages; I will go to those who are at rest, who dwell safely, all of them dwelling without walls, and having neither bars nor gates, *To take a spoil, and to take a prey*; to turn thine hand upon the desolate places that are now inhabited, and upon the people that are gathered out of the nations, who have gotten cattle and goods, who dwell in the midst of the land (Ezek. 38:8, 11-12).

There can be little doubt as to the identity of these invading hordes. Prophetic scholars have long identified them as

Russia and her satellites. Many confirming evidences are cited in support of this position; however, there is little need to explore them here in the light of the clarity of the prophetic word: "And thou shalt come from thy place out of the north parts [uttermost parts of the north], thou, and many peoples with thee..." (Ezek. 38:15). It follows logically that the people living in the uttermost parts of the inhabited area to the north of Israel are in the Soviet Union. Historical development of their passionate desire to control the Middle East serves to verify the accuracy of the prophet's words.

Russia's future invasion of the Middle East will be fully explored in another chapter. What we wish to do at this point is identify the existence of a lure which will finally prove irresistible to Russia's lust to ravish the region.

Oil, of course, is known as one of the prime attractions in the Middle East. All industrial nations are acutely aware of the vital necessity of sustaining a constant flow of the black lifeblood, which will insure positive economic possibilities. There is another consideration, however, which is often overlooked in discussions dealing with Soviet intent to control Israel and her neighbors.

Grave warnings predicting the probability of global famine are being sounded with increasing frequency these days. The question is raised, How long can our speck of earth continue to supply food for an exploding population? We will all soon be aware of the fact that, in the end, fertilizer will be as strategic a commodity as oil, or gold for that matter. Therefore, possession of adequate and readily available supplies of growth-inducing agents will be increasingly important to the great powers.

With this in mind, let us consider carefully statements made recently in Israeli publications:

> Israel is one of the few countries in the world possessing deposits of the principle raw

> materials — phosphates and potash — *for the*
> *three main types of fertilizers in common use.*[3]

> The fact that Israel produces both potash and
> phosphate gives the country an advantage
> among the world's fertilizer producers.[4]

Communist bloc countries have always been plagued with an inability to produce adequate foodstuffs for the people under their domination. Consequently, they have bowed to the embarrassing necessity of turning to capitalistic nations to fill the gap. The mineral wealth of Israel will appear to provide a vital element in the Russian quest to be catapulted to a position of global supremacy.

Jerusalem

One cannot conclude comments on the return of the Jewish people to their homeland without touching Jerusalem. It is the spiritual, intellectual, and emotional hub of Jewry. No people in history have universally yearned to possess a city as have the Jewish people. To the nations of the world, it would be a place to conquer. The ancient warriors sacked or embellished it for the glory of the empire or their sovereign. To the Crusaders, it represented a quixotic era which was designed to expel the infidel and establish a Christian kingdom complete with moated replicas of medieval European fortresses. Arab Moslems have ever regarded it as a place which held the distinction of being ranked third religiously, behind Mecca and Medina.

Thus, over the long centuries of her history, Jerusalem had been exploited, taxed, reigned over, mutilated, and camped on. Now eager Jews awaited the long-desired day when they could, once again, embrace her. Two decades later, that day would arrive.

...Jerusalem shall be trodden down by the Gentiles, until the times of the Gentiles be fulfilled (Lk. 21:24).

Jesus Christ, 30 A.D.

...We have returned to Jerusalem never to part from her again.

Moshe Dayan,
June 7, 1967

CHAPTER SEVEN

WE ARE AT THE WALL

O N A SULTRY NIGHT in mid-July, 1948, David Shaltiel gazed through the darkness at the stately ramparts of the Old City of Jerusalem. The commanding general of Haganah forces in the city was a bitterly disappointed and frustrated man. He had made promises to his troops and the Jewish people that would not be kept. Youthful officers had listened intently to his words with eyes fixed on the Israeli flag he held before them. "Tomorrow morning, this flag of Zion will fly from the Tower of David," he said. Some of these same soldiers later heard him rehearse a speech in which he would announce the liberation of all of Jerusalem and its official return to Jacob's sons and daughters. But this was a speech prepared before its time. The assaults of his determined forces on the Old City would be brutally repelled by the Arab defenders. Shaltiel was finally forced to acknowledge that the last opportunity to reach his highest objective had slipped away. The garland which he passionately desired for himself and his young, battle-weary veterans would be reserved for other brows.

Mixed Emotions

Following the War of Independence, Jewish people were ecstatic over the establishment of the state of Israel. Yet, with all of their amazing accomplishments fully tabulated, a satisfactory total could never be registered so long as the beloved city was in the hands of Ishmaelites. Israel was a nation whose heart was held by another — a condition which would endure for 20 years.

It is impossible to rationally assess the surpassing love of the Jewish people for Jerusalem. The Western world has no comparative analogy with which to liken it. Let it suffice to say, Jerusalem is as much a part of the Jewish anatomy as blood, bone, and sinew. The Psalmist said it for all Jewish generations:

> If I forget thee, O Jerusalem, let my right hand forget her cunning. If I do not remember thee, let my tongue cleave to the roof of my mouth, if I prefer not Jerusalem above my chief joy (Ps. 137:5-6).

Again, he counsels:

> Walk about Zion, and go round about her; number the towers thereof. Mark ye well her bulwarks, consider her palaces, that ye may tell it to the generation following (Ps. 48:12-13).

It is a phenomenon without historical parallel: the Jews of the far-flung Diaspora never forgot the Holy City.

The poststate years proved a trial for Jerusalemites and world Jewry as well. When the Arab Legion slammed the door in the faces of David Shaltiel's onrushing worthies, it remained sealed for two long decades. During this period, Jordan held the Old City by force in direct defiance of the United Nations' Partition Plan. Jews were expelled from their homes and denied access to their synagogues. Most traumatic was the exclusion of rights to worship at the Western Wall, the most hallowed spot on earth to the Jew, apart from the Temple Mount itself. As if to add insult to injury, the Muslim intruders systematically destroyed synagogues in the Jewish Quarter, many of which had stood for centuries. Jewish cemeteries were defiled and vandalized, homes looted, and the quarter generally desecrated.

Felt above all else was the knowledge that the sacred Temple Mount was possessed by interlopers. It was to the crest of revered Moriah that Abraham had brought Isaac on a sacrificial pilgrimage long ago. Here David had stood before the avenging angel, and so stayed the ravaging plague. Later, David, as sovereign head of the Jewish state, purchased this summit from Araunah the Jebusite as a site for the national house of worship. His son, Solomon, directed construction of the initial structure which would forever sanctify the Temple Mount as ground most holy. The Temple experienced the destructive maliciousness of the invading Babylonians before being restored by the returning exiles. Herod the Great replaced this Temple with one so magnificent that it beckoned pilgrims from the far reaches of the empire. The destruction of this edifice brought on a national state of mourning which endures to this day.

So, while the Jewish people were firmly entrenched in what came to be known as the New City of Jerusalem, a bustling center of official and commercial activity, there was a sense in which they still stood, flag in hand, forlornly viewing the walls and awaiting the opportunity to raise their ensign over the city of David.

The Coming Temple

Among the great prophetic trumpet sounds of the Old Testament is the announcement of the building of a new

Temple in the future. This Temple, says the prophet, will be constructed for the triumphant Messiah during the coming Millennial Age. It will stand as a center of memorial worship to all of the Messiah's finished work. This house of worship is described at some length in chapters 40-44 of Ezekiel's prophecy. It is to this Temple that the full manifestation of the glory of Jehovah, which had departed before the Babylonian invasion, will return. Ezekiel describes the event.

> Afterward, he brought me to the gate, even the gate that looketh toward the east, And, behold, the glory of the God of Israel came from the way of the east; and his voice was like a noise of many waters, and the earth shined with his glory (Ezek. 43:1-2).

As fervently as many elements in Jewry desire a reconstruction of the Temple on Mount Moriah, it must be acknowledged, on the best available authority, that there are no present plans to build a Jewish Temple there. The only proper place on which a Temple can be constructed is currently occupied by the Moslem Dome of the Rock. To be sure, some have sought to assist the prophetic problem by attempting to destroy the Dome. There is one reported plot in which members of the Irgun, a contingent of the assault force attacking the Old City in 1948, planned to proceed immediately to the Temple Mount and destroy the mosque in order to prepare for the construction of a new Temple. Although this story is disputed by numerous Israeli officials interviewed by the author, it was reported as factual in a major publication.[1]

While current stories of stones for a new Temple being secretly cut out and stored in hidden caves hold great fascination for many people, it can be said conclusively that there is no factual basis for these reports at this time. Some see the existence of the Temple found in the Revelation during the days of Israel's tribulation as evidencing the necessity of this clandestine sort of preparation being carried on. There is every reason to believe, however, that the structure occupying Moriah at this time might be of tabernacle type in construction and could, therefore, be raised in a short time.

There has been some confusion about the Great Synagogue now under construction adjacent to the Rabbinical Center in the New City. There is no intention for this synagogue to serve as a new Temple. Officials explain that it is to be a central synagogue and no more.

Voices in the Night

Twenty years after David Shaltiel's hour of disappointment, other eyes would survey the night-shrouded parapets of the city wall. It was near midnight as two men stood in quiet conversation outside a military command post in Jerusalem. One was a solemn-appearing, bearded rabbi. His companion, a short-statured man, stood ramrod straight, looking every ounce the soldier he in fact was. They were reviewing what had occurred in the past 48 hours — events which, when fully disclosed to the outside world, would have a stunning impact. One would find it necessary to return to the days of Joshua to find a period which even remotely approached what was taking place during the Six-Day War. The storied engagement at Jericho, with its tumbling walls, seemed almost routine by comparison. During this conflict, little Israel would be pounced upon by Arab forces on three fronts. Once again they were outgunned, outmanned, and faced by foes who promised to drive them off the land. One observer gives us a concise summary of the final outcome:

> By a feat of arms unparalleled in modern times,
> the Israelis, surrounded by enemies superior
> in quantity and quality of equipment and
> overwhelmingly superior in numbers, had
> fought a war on three fronts and not only
> survived but had won a resounding victory.[2]

The Chief Army Chaplain, Schlomo Goren, looked at Major General Uzi Narkiss, Central Commander of Israeli forces. "Uzi, you are doing great things now. What is going on in the Sinai and on the Golan Heights is nothing compared to what you are doing here in Jerusalem. I want you to remember this, when you go to the Wall I want to be with you."

Narkiss replied, "Okay rabbi, go look for a ram's horn [shofar]!"

The next morning the general was awarded one of those elusive second chances of which so many dream and so few are afforded. He was to direct the attack that would deliver Jerusalem back to its rightful heirs. It was difficult for him to grasp the fact that this was really happening. Today, General Narkiss makes no secret of his initial disappointment over the assignment given him at the outset of the Six-Day War. Orders were for him to maintain a purely defensive posture in his area. The great concern of the Israeli high command was the security of the enclave on Mount Scopus and, more particularly, the fear that a determined assault by the Arabs might cut the country in half and divide Jewish forces. His orders were clear: He was to refrain from any offensive action. Defense was the overriding objective. No one really expected King Hussein of Jordan to mount an attack along the Jerusalem perimeter. General Narkiss believes the greatest miracle of the Six-Day War was not the Jewish success in winning the Old City but, rather, the fact that Hussein attacked at all. Of course, what the general did not know at the time was that the Jordanian monarch had been deluded by Nasser's overblown estimates of imagined Arab victories. Coupled with this was the intense pressure being put on the king by his own military commanders who were itching to get into the fight. The resultant events would present the Jewish people with an opportunity which had been prayed for over two millennia, and one Uzi Narkiss had fervently hoped for since the War of Independence.

He had been among the assault forces during the futile attempts to win the Old City in 1948. At the time he was a 23-year-old leader of Palmach forces in Jerusalem. It was his group which had taken Mount Zion and successfully broken into the Old City through the Zion Gate. Ever so briefly, a corridor was opened to the Jews besieged inside the Jewish Quarter. In response to his call to David Shaltiel for support troops, he had received an assortment of bakers, shopkeepers, and townspeople who were the best Shaltiel could provide at the time. The young Palmachnik was faced with an agonizing decision — keep his exhausted troops in the city and risk losing everything, or withdraw to defend Mount Zion and maintain a strategic advantage. He decided to withdraw, a decision which would be denounced by some critics. Within hours, however, their opposing views would be all but expunged from the memories of the people, and Uzi Narkiss would step into a very select circle of Jewish luminaries.

The official order to take the Old City was issued at 6 a.m., Wednesday, June 7th. The Deputy Chief of Staff, Major General Haim Ben Lev, phoned Narkiss with the order. Narkiss, in turn, called a brigade commander, Colonel Mordechai "Motta" Gur, and charged him with the historic responsibility of taking Jerusalem.

Uzi Narkiss, Moshe Dayan, and Yitzhak Rabin at the Wailing Wall
Courtesy Israeli Embassy

One of those strange quirks of war had brought Gur and his brigade of reservists to Jerusalem. On Monday, these paratroopers had been assembled at an airfield ready to board aircraft for a drop in the Sinai. Instead, they were ordered to Jerusalem and their appointment with destiny.

Gur's morning's work involved two objectives: secure the Mount of Olives; take the Old City. With backs exposed to Arab rifles positioned on the city walls, the paratroopers rushed headlong up the side of the Mount of Olives. The sheer boldness of their assault sent the Jordanian defenders reeling. Shortly after 8:30 in the morning, the brigade commander stood before the Inter-Continental Hotel on the summit. Before him, shimmering in the brilliant rays of the morning sun, lay the city of David. The domes of El Aksa and the Mosque of Omar were dominant against the white esplanade of the Temple Mount. To the right and beyond stretched the ancient quarters: Christian, Jewish, Moslem, and Armenian. Further still, nearer the horizon, Gur's comrades in arms could see the familiar skyline of the New City. The ageless walls, so solidly constructed by the stonemasons of Suleiman the Magnificent, framed Old Jerusalem with a grandeur which moved the young soldiers with a depth of feeling which none has since been able to fully communicate. Hearts quickened as they grasped the fact — today, the two Jerusalems would become one!

It was to be a rare day in history, a day for making historic statements. Gur called for his wireless transmitter and summoned the attention of all battalion commanders. Tension rose in his voice as he spoke: "The Temple Mount, the Western Wall, the Old City. For two thousand years our people have prayed for this moment. Let us move forward — to victory."[3]

The race was on. Jewish battalions converged on the city with a collective obsession — to be the first inside and to the holy places. It was a scene reminiscent of David's mighty men storming the walls of the old Jebusite stronghold long years ago. Colonel Gur joined the chase. Leaping into his command half-track, he excitedly flung an order at his hefty, bearded driver, Ben Tsur. He ordered Tsur to get to the walls as quickly as possible. No soldier in history has responded to a command with more daring abandon than did Gur's Israeli driver. Impervious to danger, he sped down the Mount of Olives and pushed the accelerator to the floor as they began the ascent to the walls. As they careened around lumbering tanks and past hurrying infantry, the commander shouted, waved encouragement, and urged his men onward. When the half-track reached St. Stephen's (the Lions') Gate, Tsur pushed the machine unceremoniously through the doors and into the narrow street. A dazed Arab sat beside the road, stunned beyond the point of hostile action. Before them stood another gate in front of which a motorcycle sat squarely in the center of the road. Scorning the possibility of its being booby-trapped, they proceeded to run over it and through the gate. Mordechai Gur and Ben Tsur had reached the Temple Mount.

It was 9:50 a.m., Wednesday, June 7, 1967.

Soon the commander was surrounded by his victorious warriors. Again he opened his transmitter. "The Temple Mount is ours. Repeat: The Temple Mount is ours."

Other hard-running paratroopers had eyes for another objective — the Wailing Wall. As they surged through the approaches to the area, they were met by Arab legionnaires with upraised hands. These would-be prisoners of war were ignored as a cry went up from the lead soldier, "The Western Wall! I can see the Wall." Soon the official word came affirming what Jewry had long waited to hear: "We are at the Wall."

Jews were assured of once again lifting their voices before
the ancient stones beside which they had prayed for
centuries.

> See the Hebrew standing there
>   Before the ancient stones.
> He lifts his voice o'er downcast eyes
>   In soft but plaintive tones.
>
> He comes here to remember;
>   He comes here to forget.
> To mourn departed glories,
>   And dream what might be yet.
>
> From memory sunken faces
>   File by in gaunt parade.
> Now comes the haughty Sabra
>   Resolute and unafraid.
>
> Symbol of the scattered tribes,
>   Great sentinel of the years,
> Emblem of all Jewry,
>   Receptacle of tears.
>
> Mute witness to her sufferings,
>   And yearnings for release —
> Give substance to the promise
>   Of Israel's coming peace.
>   E. McQ.

At 10:15 a.m., General Narkiss came through the Lions' Gate
in his Jeep. On the way in, he came upon his night visitor,
Rabbi Goren, who was walking along the side of the road.
In the crook of one arm rested a large Torah scroll. Gripped
firmly in the other hand was the shofar (ram's horn) the general
had suggested he secure. Narkiss halted the Jeep. "Rabbi,"
he called, "come, get into the Jeep and ride with me."

"No," replied the rabbi, "two thousand years we have waited. Now I am not going to the Wall in a Jeep — I'll walk."

When the commander reached the scene, he experienced strange reactions. He recalls, "It was as though I was in another world — in a cloud of happiness ... I felt a part of the whole Jewish people, who for 2,000 years had longed for this. It was an emotion far bigger than myself, bigger than the whole generation." Along with the overwhelming emotional sensations, he awakened to the realization that he "was not prepared in any way for this occasion. I stood there before the Wall and I didn't know what to do. There I was, but what should I do? Memories of Allenby's entry into Jerusalem passed through my mind. I remembered how he had waited for several days until he received instructions from his superiors. Then the entire day was given to ceremonies surrounding his entry into the city. But me, I did not know what to do. When the rabbi arrived, he knew what to do. He prayed and blew the shofar. I then seized myself and led in the singing of the national anthem, and that was all."

It was all for only one fleeting moment. A floodgate had been opened, and the very soul of Jewish joy was gushing forth. Later that day Moshe Dayan would come to the Wall flanked by Yitzhak Rabin and Uzi Narkiss. Dayan's words upon his arrival have been preserved: "We have returned to our holiest of holy places, never to be parted from it again." He later enlarged on this somewhat by saying, "We earnestly stretch our hands to our Arab brethren in peace, but we have returned to Jerusalem never to part from her again." David Ben-Gurion visited the place and declared, as he stood before the giant blocks, "This is the greatest day of my life."

So indelible was the imprint of these hours on the minds of Jewish people in other sectors of Israel, and the world around, that intervening years have not dimmed the thoughts and emotions of the day. One Orthodox Israeli's memories are typical. "I was in my tank, on the way from Jenin to the Jordan. We had paused to rest and drink some water, when someone switched on the wireless. The announcer was reading from the Psalms. 'Our feet shall stand within they gates, O Jerusalem.' He went on to say our soldiers had taken the Old City and had reached the Wailing Wall. We had known that our troops were in the city, but to hear it this way brought such a flood of joy I cannot describe. I remember looking at my commanding officer, who was a nonreligious Jew, and the tears were flowing from his eyes and down his face."

On June 27th, the Knesset passed bills annexing the Old City. It was now official: Jerusalem was reunified under Israeli control. The flag of Zion would fly over the Tower of David at last. A few days before this took place, June 14th, a quarter of a million Jews from all parts of the country had joined a mass pilgrimage, entering through the Dung Gate, then on to the Wailing Wall. It was the largest Jewish gathering there in 2,000 years. It was a singular testimonial to the far-reaching implications of the events of the era.

Israel's friends, who were literally on the edge of their chairs in hushed, collective anxiety, lifted a sigh of relief and leaned back to survey the full scope of the incredible accomplishments of those dramatic days. Once again the young nation, sling in hand, had faced the plodding colossus and, with precise aim and audacious courage, sent the aggressors crashing down in defeat.

> Little David stood one day
>> Before a glowering foe.
> Trembling brothers watched from far
>> To see him come to woe.

Sang his sling with high-pitched note
    As stone launched from its seat.
Soon a quivering despot's form
    Lay at the stripling's feet.

Little Israel stood one day
    Before an enemy,
Who boasted loud and promised all
    He'd drive her to the sea.

Midst turbine's whine and surging tanks,
    With charging infantry,
David's sons brought down their foe
    And rewrote history.

                E. McQ.

By any standard of measurement it was an astounding feat — actually almost inexplicable. By and large, the feeling expressed by those touched by this historical lightning shaft is conveyed in a simple statement: "God was with us." It may be argued that victorious people nearly always feel this to be true. Winners instinctively believe God to be on their side and against the hapless adversaries. As results have too often demonstrated, this is most certainly not always, or probably not often the case. In this instance, however, there is just cause to carefully ponder the statement.

We have examined previously the prophetic declarations regarding the return of Israel to the land in the last days. The prophecy, as we have witnessed in our lifetime, is a living reality. Now we shall isolate the statement of Jesus Christ when He spoke prophetically of Jerusalem. Jesus had startled His followers by telling them that the splendor of Herodian Jerusalem would soon be no more; the Temple, He said, would be leveled and the Jewish people sold and driven out of the land and into the midst of the Gentile nations. Then He added:

...And Jerusalem shall be trodden down by the Gentiles, until the times of the Gentiles be fulfilled (Lk. 21:24).

Jesus emphasized the literal historical aspects of Jerusalem's deliverance from Gentile domination at His second advent. Reunification of the city in 1967 illustrates the historical momentum now moving us toward that great day.

Consider Christ's remarkable statements about events which would dominate Jerusalem's future history.

1. He predicted Jerusalem would remain under Gentile control for an undetermined period of time.

2. He further gave us to understand this condition of Gentile dominance would continue until the closing phase of history, as we have known it, was ushered in.

3. The Jewish people would become a dominant factor in end-time Jerusalem.

4. This, and related events, would mark the beginning of the end for Gentile world supremacy.

Add four additional components to the picture:

1. Christ's prediction of the fall of Jerusalem was literally fulfilled.

2. Christ's declaration concerning the destruction of the Temple was literally fulfilled.

3. Christ's prophecy concerning the dispersion of Jewry was literally fulfilled.

4. Christ's references to Israel's return to Palestine are being literally fulfilled.

Computing the Sum

It hardly seems logical or possible that were Christ an imposter and pretender, Jehovah would dignify His prophetic pronouncements with such meticulously precise historical fulfillment. As a matter of fact, one of the ultimate tests of the credentials of one who claims to be a prophet of God is the accuracy of his long-range predictions. Even the most cunning religious charlatans and well-meaning but deluded messiahs have universally failed at this point. God causes it to be so and clarifies this through the Scripture:

> And you may say in your heart, 'How shall we know the word which the LORD has not spoken?' When a prophet speaks in the name of the LORD, if the thing does *not come about or come true,* that is the thing that *the LORD has not spoken.* The prophet has spoken it presumptuously; you shall not be afraid of him (Dt. 18:21-22, NASB).

As this touches Jesus Christ, we must remember what was involved. He asserted that He was the fulfillment of all messianic prophecies of the Old Testament. There is no mistaking His declarations and understanding that He deliberately presented Himself as being one with the Father and the long-promised Son and Messiah. From that point, He moved on to predict prophetic events which would not be revealed for centuries to come. The majority of the prophecies listed above have been fulfilled since the reestablishment of the nation — several as recently as the June war in 1967. God did not frustrate the prophecies coming to pass. One by one, they were fulfilled in every detail. Beyond any question, Jesus passed the prophet's test. When these considerations are weighed, one can readily understand why His messianic claims have been accepted by vast multitudes of Jews and Gentiles across the centuries.

But Gentiles Still Predominate

Yes, they do. The final and full realization of Christ's words are clearly associated with the future advent of the Messiah. However, what we need to grasp just now is the fact that everywhere in Scripture the Jewish people are seen to be in control of Jerusalem during the period called *the last days*. This establishes the necessity of the events which we have scanned taking place. We might say that the reunification of Jerusalem was the curtain raiser in preparation for new historical disclosures which will soon come.

We must always be extremely careful not to become so dogmatic in our interpretation of events that we become guilty of attempting to usurp divine prerogatives. No one knows in full detail what tides may yet roll over Jerusalem and the land. At this writing, control of the city of Jerusalem is not open to negotiation by Israel. If stated Jewish resolve is any true indicator, it would appear Israelis are ready to die before they will relinquish control of the beloved city. Whether Jews will be forced to acquiesce under pressure for temporary internationalization of the Old City remains to be seen. It would seem, however, with all things presently available for examination considered, that the current alignment of nations, the strategic importance of the Middle East with its vast oil reserves and mineral deposits, and the relative mood trends of the Western nations and imperialistic Communists all state we could well be witnessing the heralding of the beginning of the end. It is now clearly evident that since June 7, 1967 several important elements have become intensely identifiable. The next two chapters will detail some of these compelling manifestations.

The Years Between

For Israel, the years between June 1967 and October, 1973 were a time in which the people were caught up in a national ecstasy. An aura of invincibility rainbowed the land. A Jewish air force sergeant gave voice to this feeling in a statement made in 1971. In reply to a question about a possible military intrusion by Arab forces, he thrust out a determined chin and declared: "Let them come, we can beat them all!" Such was the mood of the times. Israelis developed a tendency to see themselves, militarily, as slightly more than human in what they could accomplish. Much of the world agreed with this assessment. The Arabs sullenly licked their wounds and faced the disquieting belief that the Jews had discovered some mystic super whammy, which they applied whenever the descendants of Ishmael mustered up the courage to violate Israel's borders.

All of this would take a sudden turn on a religious fast day late in 1973.

RECONCILIATION

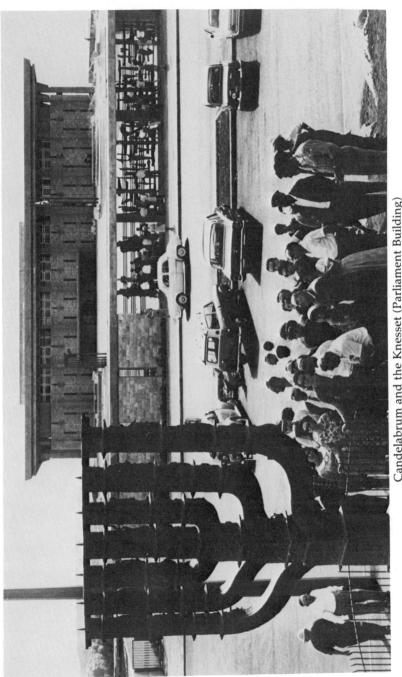

Candelabrum and the Knesset (Parliament Building)
Courtesy Israeli Embassy

On Rosh Hashanah it is inscribed and on the Fast Day of Atonement it is sealed and determined how many shall pass away and how many be born; who shall live, and who shall die; whose appointed time is finished, and whose is not....

CHAPTER EIGHT

A QUIET DAY IN OCTOBER

I F THE SIX-DAY WAR can be regarded as a modern parallel to Israel's victory at Jericho, the October War must be viewed as Israel's modern Ai. Bible readers are well-acquainted with the swift turn of events which befell Israel following the resounding victory at Jericho. Because of Israel's successes, the people of the land were trembling in fear before Joshua and his men of war. "...His fame was proclaimed throughout all the country" (Josh. 6:27).

Ai, an insignificant appearing village, was the next obstacle confronting Israel's warriors. Joshua sent men to reconnoiter and bring an estimate of the enemy's capability to wage war. Their report exuded optimism:

> And Joshua sent men from Jericho to Ai, which is beside Beth-aven, on the east side of Bethel, and spoke unto them, saying, Go up and view the country. And the men went up and viewed Ai. And they returned to Joshua, and said unto him, Let not all the people go up, but let about two or three thousand men go up and smite Ai; and make not all the people to labor there,

> for they are but few. So there went up there
> of the people about three thousand men; and
> they fled before the men of Ai. And the men
> of Ai smote of them about thirty and six men;
> for they chased them from before the gate even
> unto Shebarim, and smote them in the going
> down; wherefore the hearts of the people
> melted, and became as water. And Joshua tore
> his clothes, and fell to the earth upon his face
> before the ark of the LORD until the eventide,
> he and the elders of Israel, and put dust upon
> their heads (Josh. 7:2-6).

In view of the victory at Jericho, the report given to the commanding general of the Israeli army appeared to be sound. However, forces were moving that neither Joshua nor his informants were aware of. In fact, the cause of their impending reverses was already buried beneath the sands of Israel's own camp. They were confidently marching toward a rude awakening.

In reality they were overconfident, ill-prepared, and selling their enemy woefully short. Before the day was over, Israel's vaunted war machine experienced retreat, death, and general humiliation. The Jewish people, who waited and watched, fell under a pall of confusion and depression of spirit. The entire affair resulted in a sweeping inquiry designed to ferret out the originator of the *sin in the camp.*

Israel at Ai represents a fascinating preview of the Jewish experience during the Yom Kippur War. As was true with their ancient forerunners, they found themselves deluded by overconfidence, unprepared for the conflict, and quite unaware of the nature of the enemy's determination. In the aftermath of the war, sweeping inquiries were conducted to ascertain on whose shoulders the blame should rest. During this period sainted Israelis like Golda Meir and Moshe

Dayan became mortals again. The toll in lifeblood left on the Golan Heights and in the Sinai troubled the nation's conscience for years to come. Morale was shaken to the point that it was difficult to view the final outcome as a victory. As they scanned the horizon, a cloud of foreboding had replaced the aura of invincibility. The consequences would be far-reaching, both prophetically and politically.

The Day of Atonement

Yom Kippur is the most solemn holy day celebrated by Jews. It is a day set aside as a time of national fasting and repentance. The Day of Atonement is preceded by ten days — between the Jewish New Year's Day and Yom Kippur — of deep contrition before God. These are called "the Awesome Days." On this day Jews are to give themselves to self-examination and reconciliation with God and their neighbors. The hours of holy observance are marked by complete fasting. Everyone from 13 years of age and upward is expected to observe this solemn fast.

Yom Kippur is the one time when life in Israel comes to a near complete standstill. The religious pass the day in the synagogue wrapped in prayer shawls imploring Jehovah for forgiveness. Nonreligious Jews keep to their homes out of respect for the celebration. No shops or places of business are open on this day. Travel is forbidden. Highways are deserted of both pedestrian and vehicular traffic. Medical doctors and military personnel are the only exceptions to the stricture against travel. Radio and television do not operate on Yom Kippur. It is the one day of the year that the media fall silent.

The Day of Atonement is a day devoted to God. For a few brief hours Israel stands silent before Jehovah. The very atmosphere seems to be charged with a sense of peace and tranquility. In 1973 the day of prayer and fasting became a day for fighting and dying.

It Can't Be War

By noon on October 6th, it was apparent to worshipers that something was amiss. First, they became aware of the whine of jet engines as an increasing number of aircraft passed overhead. This was not the usual practice on Yom Kippur. Next, eyes were diverted from prayer books as cars were seen moving through the streets. The autos, some of which were stoned by religious zealots, were manned by those who were responsible for alerting military mobilization teams. Buses came later to pick up reservists from their homes for the trip to the Suez front or the Golan region.

Still, Israelis did not believe this could be war. Perhaps another of the irritating alerts which called Jews too frequently from civilian pursuits; but a full-scale war? It couldn't be.

In reality, the thing few believed could happen at this particular time was taking place. Israel had been caught by surprise. Mrs. Meir, the high command, and the officers manning the garrisons of the Bar-Lev Line, the first line of warning and defense along the Suez Canal, were all stunned and disbelieving when the Arab onslaught began. Many Jews would die without grasping the scope of the encounter. Israel was once again fighting for her existence.

One hundred ten thousand Arab troops, north and south, were poised to stream into the Promised Land. An armada of tanks and hundreds of aircraft were set to challenge Israeli armor and air strength. The massive assault was launched simultaneously on the Golan Heights and along the Suez Canal. At precisely 2:00 p.m. on Saturday, October 6th, the giant pincers began yet another attempt to impale the land.

When it became apparent to Israelis that they were involved in a struggle of major proportions, their angered query would be: How could it happen to us? How could Israel, with perhaps the most astute intelligence-gathering operatives in the world, be caught by surprise? How could preparations for such a ponderous venture be accomplished without activating red warning lights in Israel? From the human side, a number of explanations are advanced.

Golda's Choice

Prime Minister Golda Meir and the political leadership of the nation were fully aware that the Arabs were gearing for an attack on Israel at some date in the future. They were faced with whether and when to employ a first-strike offensive of the type unleashed in the Six-Day War. Israel's preemptive strike against her antagonists in 1967 had been the responsible agent in the astounding military success in that brief but decisive struggle.

However, with the first strike came the adverse winds of world opinion, with charges of Israel's being a land-grabbing warmonger. Nonetheless, with the prospective criticism well considered, Israel had few other options open. Her major population centers had been subject to the threat of almost immediate attack by adversaries in the Gaza Strip, Syrians perched on the Golan Heights, and enemies stationed within minutes of her heartland. The Six-Day War altered all of this. Now Egyptian cities would be the first to be threatened in the event of new military outbursts. The entire Sinai lay open as a base of defensive maneuver between Israel and Egypt. To the north, Syrians could be engaged at more acceptable distances from the settlements in the Valley of Jezreel. Electronic warning time for impending air attacks by the Egyptian Air Force was stretched from four minutes, prior to the Six-Day War, to 16 minutes at its conclusion. These considerations were to weigh heavily on Israel's attitude toward her ability to react when the Arabs decided to take up the fight again.

Consequently, the decision was made to allow the enemy the first blow and rely on the Israeli counterattack capability to deal with the situation. Thus world opinion would be afforded a clear view of who was attacking whom. Even when it became clear that war was brewing, Israel resisted the temptation to launch a preemptive strike. The Chief of Staff, General David Elazar, urged Mrs. Meir, Moshe Dayan, and the War Cabinet to authorize a deterrent strike during the morning of October 6th. His request was resolutely denied. Later that morning the prime minister met with Ambassador Kenneth Keating of the United States. She relayed her intelligence information which indicated an assault was inevitable, then added, "That is our decision, Israel will not open fire. Moreover, Israel is not mobilizing fully, to prevent such an act being interpreted as provocation."[1] The decision would prove a costly one.

Overconfidence

The stunning victories of the Six-Day War were to become a tranquilizing opiate to Israel. A high-ranking military official stated, in reply to the author's question about lessons learned from the Six-Day War, "We learned nothing from our victory, the Arabs learned a great deal from their defeat."

While Israeli military commanders felt confident that the tank and plane were well able to answer any future intrusion by the enemy, the Arabs were developing, under the tutelage of their Russian sponsors, deterrents to both weapons. A carefully constructed umbrella of surface-to-air missiles defused the Israeli Air Force in the opening phases of the war. The Egyptians staged their first assault to remain under the protection of their missile canopy. The success of this strategy is confirmed in the fact that the Air Force played a minimal role in the war until after the missiles were dealt with. So devastating was the effect of the Russian-made projectiles that *Aviation Week,* in its December, 1973 issue, reported that of 114 Israeli aircraft destroyed during the war, only four were lost to aerial combat. All the rest fell prey to missiles and antiaircraft.[2]

The Sagger antitank missiles, carried by infantry in suitcase-like boxes, were brought into the tank battles by both Egyptian and Syrian forces. Effective range for these weapons is one mile. They are steered to the target by trailing wires which allow the infantryman to guide it directly into the targeted tank. These fearful devices, coupled with the tidal assaults by tanks, produced vast problems for Israeli armored units. According to one report, every Israeli tank on the Syrian front was hit at one stage or another.

The Bar-Lev Line was another example of Israel's misplaced confidence. The line was composed of a series of fortifications strung along 110 miles of the Suez Canal. These installations were located seven to eight miles apart with observation posts placed at strategic points between. Tank firing ramps were constructed along the line from which armored vehicles could concentrate fire on the approaches to the Canal. At the time of the Egyptian attack, 436 Israeli soldiers manned 16 of the 33 strongholds along the line — the rest were empty. General Haim Bar Lev's creation proved of little effect as Egyptians charged through the undefended openings, thus bypassing the fortifications. Some Jews have cynically described this defense system as "Israel's Maginot Line."

Another factor which serves to emphasize Israel's unrealistic appraisal of the situation was the persistent negligence of officials to act decisively on the intelligence information, which projected ominous intentions from the Arab side. An incredible illustration of this is seen in a report that at no time before the beginning of the war "did any element link the Syrian build-up in the north...with the unusual Egyptian activity and concentrations in the south. It was as if the assumption that the Arab armies could not or would not go to war caused a complete black-out."[3]

Misinformation Maneuvers

The Egyptian Chief of Staff, Saad a-Din Shazli, is quoted from a postwar interview: "I never believed that the enemy could be led astray."[4] Neither could most of the rest of the world. But it must be acknowledged that prior to the Yom Kippur War, the Egyptians successfully laid the same trap for Israel which the Jews had sprung on them in the June War of 1967.

For years the Egyptians had labored to lull the Israelis into a condition which would allow the stage to be set for a surprise attack. Again, apparently taking a cue from the Russians, the Egyptians launched a program of *misinformation*. This process involved leaking press reports of the ineptitude and unpreparedness of their own military forces. "Expert sources" would report low morale, waste, corruption, and contention. Such reporting, done over extended periods of time, is intended to slowly sedate the enemy. A prime example of this ploy is taken from a December, 1972 release by the United Press in Brussels.

> Only 40% of Egyptian weapons and 60% of aircraft are in good working order — according to a secret Egyptian Air Force document in Cairo. Diplomatic sources in Brussels noted, as the main factors, poor maintenance and lack of spare parts from the Soviet Union. Accord-

ing to the report, Egypt has lost 50 Soviet-
made fighter planes in training since the end
of the War of Attrition. Since reputable sources
report Egypt as having 523 aircraft before the
War of Attrition, it follows that she now has
between 400 and 500, of which only 300 are
fit for combat.[5]

Such reports were filtered through press sources the world
over. No doubt many of them were factual. However, the
disciplined and determined offensive waged in the early
stages of the war belie their general accuracy.

Early on in the preparation for the resumption of hostilities,
Egypt's Anwar Sadat settled on a program of frequent large-
scale military exercises designed not only to train his own
troops but also to lure his enemy into a state of complacency.
For three years the Egyptians drilled soldiers in canal-
crossing procedures. When the crossing was finally made
on the opening day of the war, it was accomplished in
precisely the same way Israeli observers had seen it practiced
many times before. In the spring (April-May), and again in
September 1973, the Egyptians performed large-scale
maneuvers to which Israel was forced to respond by placing
armed forces on alert. When the attacks were not forthcoming, Israelis began to become wary of unnecessary
mobilization of troops at every training exercise of the Arabs.

Israel's wily adversaries rightly concluded that the
Israelis would be reluctant to call up their soldiers in view
of the soon-to-come elections, when a sense of security
is a desirable situation politically. Furthermore, in October
Israel would be observing her high holy days. Officials
would be hesitant to disrupt the observance without certain
cause to do so.

As the fateful hour of invasion approached, Arabs watched and waited while Israel swallowed the bait.

In the final analysis, no one can explain with certainty why Israel was surprised. It does seem that there was an inexplicable partial blindness upon her leadership during this period — a blindness that, when lifted after Israel's final recovery and subsequent victory, would give way to a vision embodying very solemn dimensions.

THE STORM

Death at the Waterline

The fury of war descended with deafening suddenness on both the Syrian and Egyptian fronts. Along the Canal, 2,000 Arab guns spewed 3,000 tons of devastation at Israeli fortifications in the first 53 minutes of battle. It is estimated that in the first 60 seconds of the bombardment 10,500 shells fell on Jewish positions. At the same time, 70,000 men prepared to storm into the Sinai while thousands of tanks were warming their engines for the task ahead. In preparation for the assault, giant water cannon were systematically carving gaps in the 130-foot ramparts which had been constructed by the Egyptians to hide their preparations from prying Israeli eyes. Within minutes pontoon bridges and assault boats were in the water, and soon Egyptian infantry and armor were pouring across the canal Moshe Dayan had once called the best antitank ditch in the world. Eight thousand infantrymen made up the first wave of invaders. Contesting their crossing were the 436 Israelis occupying the positions on the Bar-Lev Line. Within 24 hours five divisions of Egyptian infantry and armor would be in position three miles east of the canal.

In the air, 240 Egyptian planes flew over the bridgehead to rake Israeli airfields and missile installations in the Sinai.

Those young Israelis manning the fortifications on the line fought with the characteristic tenacity and raw courage that has so distinguished the warriors of modern Israel. It was soon apparent that their situation was militarily hopeless, and Herculean efforts were made to rescue those who were besieged in the fortifications. Distraught defenders saw Phantom and Mirage jets systematically fall to the enemy's missiles. Tanks and half-tracks attempting to reach them were set ablaze by the surface-to-surface missiles. Some of the men finally managed to escape to the safety of Israeli lines; others died defending their positions. Those who remained faced the uncertainties of captivity. Only one of the Bar-Lev strongholds managed to survive the assaults made against it.

For what seemed an interminable 48 hours, the Israelis fought a frantic holding action while they awaited the arrival of mobilized reserves. Problems were encountered in moving troops and armor to the front. The massive nature of the Egyptian invasion did not allow for much preparation or organization. Units were thrown into the fight as soon as they arrived upon the scene. The intensity of those early hours of the struggle caused an Israeli officer, Colonel Amnon, to exclaim, "The whole of Sinai was on fire."[6]

The Egyptian army that crossed the bridges into the Sinai was a new model. They were tenacious, disciplined, and well led. This army fought courageously in the face of determined Israeli opposition. Wave after wave of infantry and tanks swept into the teeth of Israeli weaponry. Even after their attack faltered, they mounted five to six new attacks daily in an attempt to dislodge Jewish forces.

When the first day's casualty figures were tabulated, the Israelis began to understand the gravity of the situation facing the nation. Five hundred of her sons were dead, a thousand more had suffered wounds. Scores of others were held prisoner. In the Six-Day War a total of 850 fell during the entire struggle on all fronts. It was soon apparent that Israel was facing her severest test in 25 years of independence. One writer has graphically summed up the problem.

> In less that 24 hours, Israel was transformed from a military power, even in global concepts; from a state with an army the fame of which had become a model to the world; from a country which — six short years ago — had won the most brilliant victory in the history of modern warfare; from a state with, according to her leaders' declarations, "an army that has never been in a better state" — to a country fighting with clenched teeth for its very existence. A country living under the shadow of extermination.[7]

By October 9th, Egyptian forces had reached the high-water mark of their drive into Sinai. Israel was by that time fully deployed and prepared to deal with the intruders. The armies were facing each other along a front which had been established some five to seven miles from the canal. On October 10th, it was decided that a crossing of the canal by Israeli forces would be the most effective way to upset the Egyptian strategy and allow Israel's tank force to employ its famous flair for speed and maneuver. Preparations began for the crossing into Egypt.

On Sunday morning, October 14th, the Egyptians launched an attack which would result in one of the largest tank battles in the history of warfare. Approximately 2,000 tanks would be engaged along the length of the front. The Egyptians came on in orderly fashion, which allowed the Israelis, with their superior range weapons, to reap havoc on them. The first Egyptian tank brigade was destroyed with a loss of 93 tanks. In this incredible battle, not one Israeli tank was lost to Egyptian armored fire. The Twenty-first Egyptian Division had 110 tanks destroyed. Major portions of Egypt's Third and Fourth Divisions met as grim a fate. By day's end, 264 Egyptian tanks lay smoldering on the desert. Only six Israeli tanks were knocked out. The tide had turned.

In the late hours of October 16th, Jewish paratroopers stood in the moonlight looking down on the waters of the Suez Canal. Ten days after Egypt had opened the war, Israel was ready to launch an invasion of her own. The crossing into Egypt would alter the entire situation and in the end accomplish the entrapment of the Third Army. This marauding force destroyed missile installations along the Canal and, in so doing, allowed the Israeli Air Force mastery of the skies over Sinai. Their triumphs would prove to be Israel's chief bargaining weapon after the cease-fire. By October 29th, Jewish troops were threatening the approach to Cairo, sealing off the dejected Third Army, and holding 16,000 square kilometers of Egyptian territory. It was now clearly time for the Russians and the United Nations to save Egypt once more.

In the Vale of Tears

Hundreds of disquietingly eerie "cats'-eyes" danced through the moonlight falling on the Golan Plateau. The "cats'-eyes" were infrared lights attached to the sides of the Syrian tanks which rumbled in orderly procession toward the Israeli positions on the Golan Heights. It was now apparent that the Syrians, who had begun their attack earlier in the day, had no intention of allowing hard-pressed Jewish troops any respite during the night. The situation facing the Northern Command of the Jewish Defense Forces was clearly perilous.

Only hours before, a United Nations observer positioned on a road situated between the territories held by Israel and Syria had witnessed a startling sight. It appeared to him as though a veritable sea of Russian-made, Syrian-manned tanks were approaching his outpost. As they neared the observation position, they veered away north and south, and one segment moved toward Kuneitra, a point roughly in the center of the Israeli defense line. The other column sped away to the south in the direction of the village of El Al in the Southern sector of the defense line. What the astonished U.N. observer was actually seeing was but two segments of the three-pronged Syrian offensive. The prearranged destinations of these armored spearheads were the bridges across the Jordan in the fertile Valley of Huleh. Their plan was to dissect the Israeli defenders in the process, slash the region into three isolated segments, and then hammer each into submission.

The Golan Heights occupies an area immediately south of Mount Hermon and northeast of the Sea of Galilee. It extends to the Yarmuk Valley in the south and to the Ruqqad Stream in the east. The Golan Plateau is a volcanic elevation which rises from 600 feet in the southern extremity to 4,000 feet in the north. The land area of the Golan Heights totals 480 square miles. These heights rise sharply from the valley floor adjacent to the Sea of Galilee. The incline is so abrupt that only a few roads permit access to the upper elevation. Israel considers possession of the area overlooking the Galilee as an indispensable necessity for the security of the villages below. It was from these heights that the Syrians, prior to 1967, lobbed shells on farmers working in the fields below. Of the main approaches from the heights, one runs through El Al. The other, and more historic route from northern

Moshe Dayan on the west side of the Suez Canal, October, 1973
Courtesy Israeli Embassy

Galilee to Damascus, crosses the Jordan at the Benot Jacov Bridge (The Bridge of the Daughters of Jacob). This road runs through Kuneitra on the main route to Damascus.

Militarily, the problems of defending the Golan Heights differ drastically from those faced by forces in the Sinai. From the Suez Canal to the centers of population in Israel lay 125 miles of desert. This allows for defensive retreats while awaiting reservists to mobilize and deploy. Only 17 miles of virtually unbroken plain, with no naturally defensible barriers, stood between the Syrians and the steep cliffs descending from the Heights prior to the war. Israeli and Syrian troops were separated by a no-man's-land some one-half to one mile wide running the length of the Purple Line, which marked the cease-fire line established following the June '67 war. United Nations observers occupied posts along the main routes between the opposing forces.

Israel had established 17 fortifications, each manned by 15 troops, along the Purple Line. These fortifications ran from Mount Hermon to the Yarmuk River. The installations were well dug in, protected by mines and wire obstacles. Behind these a detachment of tanks was stationed. The system was designed to effectively block a Syrian advance until reserves could be mobilized. The assumption was that intelligence would provide adequate time for preparation and mobilization. This would not be the case. A second assumption was that massive air support would be available to support the holding action during the initial phases of hostilities.

One of the key factors in the defense of the Golan was the Jewish outpost located on Mount Hermon. The position was an electronic observation station 6,600 feet up the side of the mountain. From it, Israelis commanded a view of the entire battle area. The loss of this position and its sophisticated equipment in the early stages of the fighting was a major blow to the Israeli effort.

When the fighting began, matters were further complicated by the presence of civilians who lived in 15 settlements on the plateau. Eleven were within a few miles of the cease-fire line. By noon Saturday women and children had been evacuated from the settlements. However, the men had remained and were there when the attack came. Their evacuation impaired the combat units' effectiveness during the early hours of the war.

The first wave of 300 Syrian tanks which had startled the U.N. observer moved ponderously about their appointed tasks. As the column divided and swung toward the respective targets, another 400 tanks moved up from the south along the road to Raphid. One hundred seventy-six Israeli tanks braced to meet the steel-tracked armada's onslaught. Sight of the parade ground approach of the Syrian force caused one waiting Israeli to exclaim: "I never knew there were so many tanks in the whole world."[8] Syria's plan of attack called for a 55-minute artillery barrage followed by an armored assault of such superior weight of numbers that the Jewish defenders would be overwhelmed as the attackers moved toward the bridges on the Jordan.

Of the bridges spanning the Jordan in this area, it appears relatively certain two were marked for crossing by what the Syrians intended to be a triumphal entry into Israel. One was the Benot Yacov Bridge, by way of Kuneitra. The other was the Arik Bridge and spanned the river just north of the tip of the Sea of Galilee. Overall objectives of the invaders envisioned completing destruction of all Israeli opposition on the Golan Heights by Tuesday, October 8th.

The southerly thrust was met by the Barak Brigade and contingents from the Seventh. On the morning of October 6th, the commander of the brigade found members of his command absorbed in fasting and prayer. The group was being visited by an orthodox Hasidic group whose zeal had persuaded even the nonreligious soldiers in the unit to join in the solemn rituals. As he listened, the brigade commander was moved by the prayer being recited by his troops: "On Rosh Hashanah it is inscribed and on the Fast Day of Atonement it is sealed and determined how many shall pass away and how many shall be born; who shall live, and who shall die, whose appointed time is finished, and whose is not...."[9]

Over the next few days 90 percent of the tank commanders in the Barak Brigade were killed or wounded. Jewish tank commanders directed action from partially exposed postures with hatch open and upper bodies in the open.

The saga of the Barak Brigade is one of singular heroism in the face of irresistible odds. By the time the first day and night of fighting ended, the Barak Brigade had been reduced to a force of 15 functioning tanks. Still they repeatedly flung themselves into a path of 450 Syrian tanks.

Acts of individual heroism abounded. Among the most conspicuous were the exploits of a young Israeli, Zvi "Zwicka" Greengold. The freckled blond lieutenant made his home on a kibbutz in western Galilee. He was on leave when news of the outbreak of fighting reached him. Hitchhiking north, he arrived at the command headquarters at Nefekh and asked for a command. The request was granted, and he was given four tanks, three of which had to be repaired before being fit to see action. His group was named "Force Zwicka" and sent into the fray. Over the next 30 hours Zwicka would reap havoc on the enemy. When the other tanks in his command were destroyed, he fought alone engaging one of the main thrusts of the Syrian advance. Opposing forces outnumbered him at a fifty-to-one ratio. Through the night he darted in and out among the hills to destroy enemy tanks, then quickly melted into the night.

At one point his tank was hit and set afire. Zwicka flung himself to the ground, wounded and suffering burns on his face and arms. Recovering from the initial shock of his wounds, he commandeered a passing tank and, scrambling through the hatch, continued his war. Before Zwicka dragged his battered body from his tank with a muttered apology to his superior officer, "I can't anymore," Zvi Greengold, son of survivors of the Holocaust, had single-handedly, according to figures given by his officers, destroyed 60 Syrian tanks.

Despite such heroic efforts, the Syrian assault moved on and took up a position on the outskirts of El Al, one of their objectives on the road south. The invaders were apparently stunned by their successes. They had broken effective Israeli resistance. At the moment, the bridge on the Jordan was wide open to them. Strangely, however, at this point *they stopped*. No one can explain why. Perhaps, as with the Egyptians, their successes had made them wary for fear the Jews had baited a trap for them. It could be they went only as far as initial strategy outlined and then stopped to await further instructions. When they halted the advance on the night of the 6th, their lead tanks were within four to six miles of the Jordan River. By the time they prepared to continue the offensive, Israeli reserves were on the scene ready to block the advance. Viewing the situation, one incredulous Israeli soldier quipped: "The Syrians simply stopped in mid-stream, and didn't start again. Why? We'll ask them sometime, if we have the chance."[10]

To the north, the Seventh Brigade was being hammered by successive waves of assaulting armor. This Brigade was born in the battles of Latrun during the War of Independence. The Seventh had long been established as one of the premier fighting units of the Israeli Defense Forces. Their present task was to block the attempt by the Syrians to penetrate along the Damascus to Kuneitra road — the most direct access route to the Benot Yacov Bridge. The Syrians' first attempts to cross the antitank ditch prepared by the Israelis were repulsed at a fearful cost to the aggressors. Although the Jews were satisfied with the performance of their armored forces in this encounter, they were deeply concerned over the persistence of the enemy and the weight of the forces driving into the central sector. As successive columns of tanks exploded under the impact of Israeli shells, the Syrian force simply kept coming on, in what appeared to be an endless procession.

Syria had chosen a two and one-half mile swath across a valley between Hermonit Hill and a ridge called "the Booster." The Seventh Brigade was well positioned defensively at this point. In military terms, they had chosen an ideal *killing ground.* However, the odds against the defenders were prohibitive, to say the least. As 500 tanks led by Russian-made T62's, the most modern on the field, advanced in a night foray (October 7th), they were opposed by 70 Israeli tanks. Interspersed among the vehicles of Syria's steel armada were infantrymen carrying antitank bazookas. Jewish and Arab forces locked in a death struggle that raged through the night, with attacker and defender often firing at each other from point-blank range. Indeed, tanks and infantry from the two armies became intermingled in the darkness, and the battlefield became a nightmare of destructive confusion. Finally, the Syrians broke off the attack and retreated in order to regroup for a new thrust.

As morning light crept across the valley, Israelis saw the curtain rising on a ghastly scene. No less than 130 Syrian tanks lay destroyed and abandoned before them. Wrecked personnel carriers and human bodies added to this dreadful portrait of death and destruction. Exhausted Jews spoke for themselves and their adversaries when they appropriately named this sector of the struggle for the Golan Heights "The Valley of Tears."

Nor was this the end — these men fought on for days without appreciable respite. Sleep and food were luxuries which they could ill afford to indulge in. When the tanks were not rolling toward them, artillery and rockets were whooshing in on their positions.

Before the battle-drained Jewish warriors saw trailing dust columns rising from the tracks of the retreating Syrian juggernaut, hundreds of other metal and human dead gasped their last in the graveyard called "The Valley of Tears." Not only here, but across the entire Golan lay the remnants of the battle which had threatened Israel's very existence. General Raful Etyan, who was in command of all Jewish forces on the Golan Heights, spoke by way of wireless radio to Colonel Avigdor, commander of the Seventh Brigade, as the latter looked down on "The Valley of Tears." Colonel Etyan said, "You have saved the people of Israel."[11] That commendation would be handed to all courageous Jews who fought on the Golan Heights.

By war's end, Jewish defenders had successfully dealt with an attack by Jordanian and Iraqi armored forces. Occupied land area on the Heights would be enlarged appreciably and advanced columns positioned well down the road to Damascus. At a considerable cost of lives, the Golani Brigade wrested the strategic observation post on Mount Hermon from the Syrians in the waning hours of the war.

When the full tally was taken, it became obvious that Israel, north and south, had forged a remarkable victory. It was a triumph, however, which brought no festive celebrations.

Aftermath

As the brutal statistics of war began to be tabulated, the Jews of Israel and the world went into mourning.

By statistical comparison, the scope of the victory was quite obvious. The Syrians and Egyptians are estimated to have lost perhaps 16,000 men. Combined Arab forces, which included not only Syrians and Egyptians but Iraqi and Jordanian armor also, saw 2,000 tanks and 450 planes destroyed. Israel lost 800 tanks and 104 aircraft. Coupled with the land gained during the conflict, it adds up to an exceptional accomplishment.

For Israel, however, it was an unconscionably costly struggle. Two thousand five hundred and twenty-three Israelis had been killed in the fighting, while thousands more lay wounded. This was over three times the number lost in the Six-Day War. While these figures may not seem excessive from a statistical point of view — roughly about one-tenth of one percent of the population perished — they served to trigger the shock and bewilderment that seized the nation as a result of this war.

Moshe Dayan referred to this period as "a time when heroes were deposed." It was also a time when national illusions were shattered. For the first time since independence, many Jewish people saw their confidence in national leadership eroded. The military establishment, long lauded for an unparalleled capacity for preparedness, suddenly became suspect. Question marks began to rise over the commitment of allies abroad — particularly those in Europe who had offered no help to the Israelis. These elements, and others which we shall explore shortly, converged to plunge the nation into a prolonged state of depression — a condition which endured without appreciable letup until the daring rescue of the hostages at Entebbe in 1976. A Jewish woman articulated the mood to the author in late 1975. She said, "We are only now beginning to realize that we actually won the Yom Kippur War, that it was a victory rather than a defeat." These were days when the words of the prophet forced their way once again into the minds of the Jewish people: "Is it nothing to you, all ye that pass by? Behold, and see if there be any sorrow like unto my sorrow..." (Lam. 1:12).

Perhaps the extended lament raised by distraught Israelis was in part a release of pent-up tensions which had placed a strain on minds and emotions for many years. In truth, no nation had lived under the threat of potential disaster as has Israel. Volatile belligerence and seemingly inflexible dedication by the Arabs to the destruction of Israel was almost certain to cause a crack in the national nervous system at some point. Constant threats, acts of terrorism, harassment, and recurrent mobilization of armed forces to meet potential attacks all contributed to the final reaction. As Israel gathered the bodies of her young after a war callously begun on the highest of holy days, the full measure of frustration, fear, and unquenchable anger burst from Jewish hearts. However one might choose to assess and assign contributing factors, we are certain of the results. Depression, suspicion, and economic hardship were the lingering legacies of the Yom Kippur War.

Three distinct results can be singled out for comment:

Uncertainty: Israelis were not sure any longer. The sense of invincibility had vaporized. A psychologist accurately phrased the mood: "This war dispelled Israel's seeing themselves as supermen and the other side as permanently inferior and destroyed their ideas of security."

Futility: Not in the sense that Israel was ready to quit (one of the fears of Jewish leaders following the war was that the Arabs might misinterpret the mood and commit the error of launching a new offensive), but the feeling was that every new fight, even when Jews were victorious, only presaged more battles ahead. War seemed to be a horrible fact of life, one which could not be driven or prayed from their midst.

Isolation: Most significantly, from a prophetic point of view, was the settling in of an awareness of the growing feeling of being slowly isolated. There had only been one hand of help extended during the days of trauma. Major General Chaim Herzog notes in his forceful book, *The War of Atonement,* "Only the United States appreciated the significance of Israel's struggle."[12] The sight of major European nations cowering before Soviet blustering and the Arab oil sheiks caused justifiable consternation.

Since the war, more substantiating evidences have been accumulating. The ludicrous decisions by the United Nations, most noteworthy that of branding Zionism as racist and the attempt to oust Israel from the world body, have had their effect. Soviet Russia, with an iron-handed determination to dominate and eventually possess the area, pursues a transparent course of international meddling designed to isolate then subjugate Israel. (We shall explore the Russian intent in the next chapter.) Even Israel's one firm ally, the United States, is viewed with some uneasiness. There is no doubt at this point as to the overwhelming sympathy of the American people for Israel. The reaction of the U.N. decision on racism and the Entebbe raid confirm this loyalty. Yet there can be no guarantee that American leadership, which vacillated in the face of Arab economic aggression during the oil boycott, will be more resolute in the future. It is a well-known fact that America is consistently increasing its dependence on Arab oil with little impetus toward developing national resources in order to assure independence. If this trend continues and a new crisis arises, the result could stifle American industry which would inevitably touch the bread supply. When, in turn, the Arabs point in the direction of the ostensible "cause of the problem," Israel, we could witness not only a new period of retrenchment but a refueling of anti-Semitic fires.

A young Sabra, the daughter of an Israeli foreign service officer, captured the feeling of Israelis best when she answered a question about what she felt American youth could do to assist Israel. Her poignant response was: "Tell them to believe it is important for us to survive."

A Man Must Come

A Jewish historian writes of two manifestations which historically have become evident when Jews pass through times of trouble. The first, he says, is a longing to return to the ancient land of Abraham. The second is a commensurate revival of messianic expectation. In this observation, our historian is in precise agreement with the prophets of the Bible. They assert with certainty a time when Israel will occupy a place of national isolation. There will be left to them no human hand of help. No political system, military combine, or resolution of self-determination will avail to stay the hand of hostile aggressor nations. Zechariah refers to this period: "And in that day will I make Jerusalem a burdensome stone for all peoples; all that burden themselves with it shall be cut in pieces, *though all the nations of the earth be gathered together against it*" (Zech. 12:3). The central ramifications of Zechariah's words will be dealt with in a subsequent chapter. For now, we must emphasize this idea of the development of isolation which, according to the prophets, will culminate in a unified national outcry for the revelation of the Messiah.

Following the Yom Kippur War, signs of a new period of messianic expectation began to find expression. Significantly, these are to be found not only in predictable religious sources but in secular ones as well.

On the religious side are orthodox groups, of which the *Gush Emunim* movement is a clear illustration. *Gush Emunim* (a faithful bloc or a group of believers) is a settlement movement which arose after the Yom Kippur War. The majority of its adherents are religiously zealous messianic Jews who are actively preparing for the day when the Messiah will appear. Their explanation of basic beliefs is illuminating.

"When we saw how bad things became during the Yom Kippur War, we were convinced that the coming of the Messiah must be very near. So while other Jews were depressed over the outcome of the war, we were encouraged. We believe that this was the beginning of the redemption of Israel. Our belief is quite simple, really, we believe when we possess all of the land historically held by the Jewish people, the Messiah will come. How will He come? Hasidic Jews expect Him to come suddenly, miraculously, seated on a cloud. We do not believe this. Our belief is He will come to Jerusalem in a lowly manner, riding on a colt of an ass."

It is this group which has attempted to settle difficult areas on the West Bank and on the Golan Heights.

Secular Israelis are making similar statements, although they would not claim religious bias for doing so. One frequently gathers from private conversations with Jewish people from various walks of life a tone which seems to indicate a realignment of thinking — a conclusion that the hope for the future is not to be found in another system. Rather, it is to be found in the appearance of a man who can provide qualities of leadership which none, to this point in modern times, has displayed. This feeling can be demonstrated by two illustrative statements. In the home of a publisher one evening in Jerusalem, the author, the host, his family, and other guests were talking about politics and current problems. At one point in the conversation, one of the guests, a historian, rose to his feet and declared, "America has not produced a philosopher in fifty years. *A man must come,* one who can take control. A man who towers above all the rest." There was general agreement among the Jewish people present that this was the ultimate answer.

A few days later, while at lunch with a friend who holds a doctorate from the Hebrew University and occupies a position in one of the Zionist agencies, the subject of messianic expectation was again posed. He replied, "No. I don't believe there is much hope of a revival of that kind of thinking in modern Israel." Moments later, on our walk back to his office, again on the subject of politics, he offered this observation: "You know, I can't explain it, but there is great trouble ahead. I believe we will have another war, a big war with Russia. Things will be bad for awhile, but then it will be all right. Don't ask me how I know it, but I am certain it will happen this way." Without being aware of what he was saying, this young man detailed the prophetic future of the Chosen People. As we shall see, two climactic intrusions into the Middle East will hold the focus of the future. Russia will venture into the Promised Land and meet disaster. The nations will follow shortly thereafter and meet the Messiah.

In closing this chapter, it is fitting to return to our original comparison. Jericho is certainly reminiscent of the successes of the June War. Ai and Yom Kippur are compatible comparisons of humiliation and frustration, ancient and modern. But we must not stop there. If one moves on through the pages of Joshua's historical account, he will soon arrive at yet another battle. This time it was not a single adversary but a confederation of belligerent kings banded together for the sake of crushing Joshua and his Israelites (see Josh. 10:5-15). When the dust of battle settled and the day had at last been won, the inspired penman said, "And there was no day like that before it or after it, that the LORD hearkened unto the voice of a man; *for the LORD fought for Israel"* (Josh. 10:14). Israel's last great confrontation will once again see the day when the Lord will fight for His people.

The key to war in the Middle East is in the hands of the Soviets, while the key to peace is held by the United States.

Moshe Dayan

CHAPTER NINE

THE STALKING BEAR

T HE YOM KIPPUR WAR provided a graphic demonstration of the intentions of the Soviet Union. As one
views the chronicle of Russian involvement in the
struggle, there can be no doubt as to the direction in which
Russian policy is aimed — Israel and the entire Middle East.

Before we begin our consideration of the historical aspects
of the Russian scheme, we should set the stage by providing
a prophetic backdrop against which all of these factors can
be reflected. In a previous chapter a passage was drawn from
Ezekiel's prophecy which touched on the Russian desire to
take the wealth of Israel and the area in hand. Keep in mind
that these words were penned in the sixth century B.C.!

> Thus said the Lord GOD: It shall also come
> to pass that at the same time shall things come
> into thy mind, and thou shalt think an evil
> thought...And thou shalt come from thy place
> out of the north parts, thou, and many peoples
> with thee, all of them riding upon horses, a
> great company, and a mighty army; And thou
> shalt come up against my people of Israel, like

> as a cloud to cover the land; it shall be in
> the latter days, and I will bring thee against
> my land, that the nations may know me, when
> I shall be sanctified in thee, O Gog, before
> their eyes (Ezek. 38:10, 15-16).

WITH A LITTLE HELP FROM A FRIEND

The Yom Kippur War would not have been initiated had Russia not been a consenting and cooperating partner in the venture. It is a matter of record that Anwar Sadat was reluctant to begin a new escapade against Israel until a proper deterrent to the threat of Israeli deep-penetration bombing of Egyptian targets was in hand. The Soviets supplied this assurance with the delivery of Scud Battlefield Support Surface-to Surface Missiles in March of 1973. Scud missiles are capable of delivering high explosive or nuclear warheads at a range of 180 miles. This confirmed the ability to reach Jewish centers of population in the heart of Israel. Bolstered by this capacity to disseminate devastation, he made the decision to begin the war. Thus the determination to attack Israel was actually made by the Soviets when they placed the Scud in Sadat's hands.

One unconfirmed report suggests it was Kremlin planning that chose the very day when the hostilities should begin.

> The French Weekly *Le Nouvel Observateur* later
> reported that the ex-head of the Soviet military
> mission in Egypt, General Vassil Vasilevitch
> Okolkoniev, was the man who chose Yom
> Kippur as the appropriate time to surprise
> Israel: "The Russian general read that the radio
> is silent in Israel on the Day of Atonement,
> and so he thought up the idea."[1]

Those who recall the dramatic U.N. sessions following the Six-Day War, when Abba Eban read lists of Soviet military equipment which had fallen unscathed into Israeli hands, will also remember the sullen resolution written on the countenances of the Russian delegates. It was unmistakably clear to observers that there would be no rest until the sting of humiliation could be assuaged.

Rebuilding of the Arab war vehicle was undertaken immediately after hostilities ceased in the Six-Day War. On June 11, 1967 the Kremlin had urged Nasser not to quit, assuring him all of the aid necessary to recoup his losses. Only weeks afterward, a Soviet mission arrived in Egypt to evaluate problems and establish a plan to rebuild the Egyptian military force. The result was implementation of a threefold program.

Reequip: Russia would replace what Egypt had lost to the Jews. Within a brief span of six months this was, for all practical purposes, accomplished. The ultimate Soviet goal was the creation of an Egyptian army which would number 800,000 troops. This time around, Russia would supply equipment designed to deal with the two most formidable weapons the Israelis had at their command, the plane and the tank. Covering missile systems and the surface-to-surface antitank projectiles were the result of their efforts.

Train: It would not be enough for the U.S.S.R. to supply the weapons for a new war; they would also take the responsibility for fashioning a new breed of soldier — Russia would train the new Egyptian army. Every missile installation, brigade, and battalion had its own Russian advisor who kept tabs and made reports on the Egyptian officers. Soviet arrogance and thinly veiled contempt for the Egyptian soldier soon created a situation which bred deep-seated resentment among the members of the Egyptian student army. This growing attitude of hostility toward the Russians became so pronounced that Anwar Sadat, in a short-lived fit of pique after an unhappy set of exchanges with the hierarchy in the Kremlin, asked for a withdrawal of advisors and troops from Egypt. No one applauded more enthusiastically than the officers who had been belittled by the Soviets. The Russians, however, had no intention of allowing their clients to shake off the yoke, and accordingly many advisors and instructors never left the country.

Before long the differences were patched up, and the spirit of the Treaty of Friendship and Cooperation was once again operative. This treaty was a 15-year agreement whereby the Soviets pledged aid to Egypt in her building of a socialistic society.

One must concede that the Russian objectives for the armies of both Egypt and Syria were admirably successful. The one insurmountable difficulty they faced was an inability to teach the Jews how to be defeated.

Manning the Hardware: To further insure that there would be no repeat of the 1967 fiasco, Russia decided upon more direct forms of assistance for their clients. In certain instances, Russians manned the hardware they supplied.

During the War of Attrition from March, 1969 to August, 1970, the Israelis responded to massive artillery bombardments along the Suez front by sending the Air Force on deep-penetration bombing sorties against Egyptian targets. In the process they wrecked the network of Sam 2 missiles which had been carefully erected to circumvent the very thing the Israelis were accomplishing. Sadat sent out a hurried S.O.S. to the Kremlin. The response was eagerly forthcoming. Fifteen hundred Soviet personnel accompanied the Sam 3 missiles sent to replace the old system. The missiles were manned by Russian technicians. These were supplemented by the eventual arrival of an additional 15,000 to

20,000 air defense units which now bore the brunt of protecting Egypt from Israeli penetration. Of course, this meant Israel would not be contesting with her Arabic neighbors but directly involved in confrontation with Russian forces. In fact, before the War of Attrition was over Israeli jets did battle, on at least one occasion, with Russian-piloted patrols over the Suez Canal.

During the battle for the Golan Heights in the Yom Kippur War, Soviet advisors were helicoptered to the Israeli position on Mount Hermon which had fallen to the Syrian forces. Once on the scene, they did an in-depth examination of the equipment captured by the Syrians.

It is worth observing that at the time many of these things were taking place, particularly the deliveries of vast quantities of offensive weapons to both Egypt and Syria, Russia was sanctimoniously espousing the concept of détente with the United States.

A Growl From the North

Collapse of the Arab forces brought an impassioned response from the Russians — a response which brought them to the brink of direct intervention and the world to the edge of nuclear upheaval.

Time magazine, in the April 12th issue, presented an intriguing scenario of the brush with nuclear conflagration. According to the *Time* report, Israel assembled 13 nuclear devices during the early stages of the October War, when things looked bleak for the Jews. "At 10 p.m. on October 8, the Israeli Commander on the northern front, General Yitzhak Hoffi, told his superior: 'I am not sure I can hold out much longer.' After midnight, Defense Minister Moshe Dayan solemnly warned Premier Golda Meir: 'This is the end of the third temple.' Mrs. Meir thereupon gave Dayan permission to activate the Doomsday weapons."

The article further stated that by the time they were deployed, the crisis had passed and with it any further consideration of using the devices. *Time* and other sources believed Russia probably learned of Israel's nuclear weapons through observation by the Cosmos spy satellite orbiting over the Middle East.

On October 13th, Russia sent nuclear warheads to Alexandria, Egypt to be installed on the Scud missiles. The United States, however, detected these devices as the ship transporting them passed the Bosporus on October 15th. With this discovery came America's warning to the Russians through issuing a military alert.

Other reports indicate decisively that the Soviets were prepared to join the fight on behalf of the Arabs. As the situation deteriorated for the Egyptians — Jewish forces had established a bridgehead on the other side of the Suez Canal and the Egyptian armored forces had met calamity — Sadat issued a plea for joint military intervention by the U.S. and Russia. Russian satellite reconnaissance had verified the glum situation. The Soviets were ready to respond affirmatively; however, the United States refused to become involved. A Russian note reportedly sent by Brezhnev to American officials stated: "I shall state plainly that if the United States rejects the opportunity of joining with us in this matter, the Soviet Union will be obliged to examine as a matter of urgency the question of the unilateral institution of appropriate measures to stop Israeli aggression."[2]

Consequently, the Russians began a buildup which had all of the appearances of readying for a military intrusion. Soviet divisions in East Germany and Poland were placed on alert. A full division of Soviet airborne troops was transported from positions close to Moscow to an airfield near Belgrade, Yugoslavia. The staff of this division was even then in Syria, positioned just outside of Damascus. Other

Soviet units, along with Anatov freighter aircraft, were also removed to Belgrade. Southeast of Cyprus, the Russians were mounting a naval buildup complete with assault boats and helicopter pilots. Joined with these developments was the disquieting discovery by U.S. reconnaissance over Egypt of the deployment of the Scud missiles.

The United States reacted with the combat alert. All U.S. troops were placed on standby, awaiting orders. All leaves were cancelled. The alert was worldwide and involved over 2,000,000 American military personnel.

In concert with the alert, Secretary of State Kissinger drafted a communique' to Secretary Brezhnev. It stated that the United States would not abide any intervention by the Soviet Union in the Middle East. Any intrusion by the Russians, said Kissinger, would place world peace in jeopardy. The Russians backed away.

How near the world stood to a nuclear button being pushed by Israel, Egypt, or the Soviets must remain speculative. However, we were served with a vivid example of Russia's continuing obsession with expansionist ambitions.

With Eyes to the South

Keeping Ezekiel's prediction in mind, it will be instructive to trace the development of Russia's southerly thrust which will finally spend itself on the mountains of Israel. A survey of historical considerations will illustrate clearly how far we've come, where we stand at this point, and what must lie just ahead.

If one views a map of Russia in the late 1500's and compares it with present-day territory of the U.S.S.R., he will observe that over those 400 years the land area held by the Soviets has increased 16 times. History for the period teaches that the Russians have been in an almost continuous program of expansion. The fact that, of the 240,000,000 population, 112,000,000 are not Russian, serves to emphasize the point. In addition to this, since World War II Russia has forcibly annexed six independent eastern European states with non-Russian populations totaling another 105,000,000 people.

At the heart of Russia's expansionist designs has been the desire to become a naval power. Thus she first moved north in the direction which afforded least resistance, the Arctic. Next came the area bordering the Baltic which offered the nearest shore. Peter the Great established a foothold there and began building the first Russian navy. The Black Sea, held from the end of the 15th century, provided ice-free ports, but still the exits into and from the Mediterranean were controlled by other nations.

Over the centuries the Soviets have systematically moved to secure additional territories in all directions. From the 16th century until she was defeated by Japan in 1905, Russia expanded eastward into Asia. Even after this setback, until 1914, she scooped up sizable portions in these regions. Through these years Russia's efforts more or less met with success, depending on variable factors at given times. The Bolshevik Revolution (1917) saw a transition which offered her neighbors but brief respite. Communistic imperialism soon began the inexorable journey to its appointed destiny.

There are, of course, apologists who will dispute any assertion questioning Russia's intentions as less than benevolent. The most eloquent rebuttal to this defense is a look at the map. Neighbors of the U.S.S.R. are either armed and defensively stationed along the borders — as in the cases of Western Europe and China, with Iran currently making moves in this direction — or politically intimidated by the Soviet colossus. All live constantly with the specter of the comrades to the north very much in mind.

Most recently the Soviets have been occupied with movements toward the south, with eventual focus squarely on the Middle East. A secret agreement on the Middle East made by Russia and her World War I allies would have granted her control of a significant portion of the land area held today by Iran. The agreement also ceded a considerable slice of eastern Turkey to the Black Sea and authority over Constantinople (Istanbul) and the Straits into the Mediterranean. The Russian Revolution negated implementation of the agreement, but what is important is the fact that Russia had turned eyes south and was beginning to make her move in that direction. At the outset, the Bolsheviks renounced territorial aspirations. By the 1930's, however, they were clearly exploiting their power. The Communists would soon take up where the czarists left off, but before their efforts could know any measure of success, a major change was necessary; for following World War I, the Western powers were firmly entrenched in the Middle East.

The West Retreats

The year 1920 marked the zenith of Western influence in the Middle East. Algeria, Tunisia, Aden, Libya, Egypt, Iraq, Palestine, Cyprus, and the Sudan were all under direct British rule. Oman was under indirect rule, while Turkey, Persia, and what is now Saudi Arabia (except Yemen) were in alliance with the British crown.

During the years between 1921 and 1939 a period of retrenchment set in. Egypt became an independent kingdom with certain "reserved points" secured to Britain. Iraq became independent, while Transjordan became an emirate under British mandate. Turkey, Persia, and Saudi Arabia all gained independence in this period. Indeed, by 1940 the Western hold on the Middle East was slipping badly.

The years between 1940 and 1971 saw retrenchment turn into full retreat. Western predominance, especially in the case of Great Britain, was all but erased completely. Syria, Lebanon, the Sudan, Morocco, Tunisia, Algeria, Aden, and Libya joined the ranks of independent nations during this time. Also, Rhodes was ceded to Greece, the Canal Zone agreement was nullified, and the Palestine mandate abandoned. By 1971 the United States and Britain saw the area virtually swept clean of their military bases. Morocco, Algeria, Tunisia, Libya, Egypt, Iraq, and Aden all issued eviction notices to the West. Only Malta and Cyprus remained open for military operations. And while the newly independent nations were breathing the heady air of self-determination, the Soviet Union was already well along in forging her nefarious campaign to put shackles on Arab and Israeli alike.

Russia Moves In

"In 1940, Nazi Germany proposed that Russia should join the Tripartite Pact (of Germany, Italy, and Japan). The proposal centered round the idea that the three Axis powers would agree in advance to certain Soviet territorial ambitions.

"On 25 November 1940, in an official note addressed to Germany, the Soviet Government accepted the proposal in principle and defined 'the centre' of Russia's territorial aspirations as *the area south of Baku and Batum in the general direction of the Persian Gulf.*'"[3] (Batum is located on the eastern tip of the Black Sea near the Turkish border. Baku is situated on the western side of the Caspian Sea, north of Iran.)

Although Russia's alliance with the Axis powers was not consummated, after the war she made four attempts to implement her stated desires.

In March of 1945 the U.S.S.R. claimed the right to establish a permanent military base on the Dardanelles because Turkey was, in the Russian view, too weak to deter "foreign powers."

Next, the Soviets demanded that Turkey cede a strip on the southeastern tip of the Black Sea which ran along the Russian-Turkish border south to Iran. Their argument was based on Russia's possession of the area during part of the previous century.

During World War II, British and Russian troops had been stationed, by agreement, on Iranian soil. After the British withdrew according to the accepted timetable, Russia refused to evacuate her troops and kept them in the province of Azerbaijan. By the end of 1945 all key positions in government in the province were occupied by Communists, who were declaring the province independent of Iran. When Iranian troops sought to intervene, they were blocked by the Soviets and denied entrance. After the matter was brought to the U.N. on two occasions and pressure brought to bear, Russia agreed to withdraw, provided she be granted controlling interest in a Russian-Persian oil company covering all Iranian territories bordering on the Caspian Sea and the U.S.S.R. The Iranian parliament refused to ratify the agreement after Soviet withdrawal, and the Russians dropped the case.

A fourth effort was launched in September 1945. The United States, Britain, France, and China were approached by Russia with the idea that the U.S.S.R. be allowed trusteeship over Tripolitania, a sizable portion of northern Lybia adjacent to Tunisia. Her justification was that the Soviet Union needed Mediterranean ports for her merchant fleet.

Russia was turned aside in all of these efforts to seek her fortunes in the south. The important consideration to grasp is that it was the Western powers, led by a determined United States, which refused to allow the Bolsheviks to gain their objectives. While, as we have seen, many of the land bases were denied the U.S., entry of the Sixth Fleet into the Mediterranean became a primary deterrent to Soviet ambitions.

However, tyrants never sleep because tyranny is an insatiable mania, and the failure to reach stated goals only breeds a more ruthless determination to do so. History provides no clearer witness to this than the Soviet Union. Their reverses were seen as temporary frustrations which in no way diminished commitment to the broad objective. It would only be a matter of adopting new methods of approaching the problems. The next offensive was launched among the fledgling independent nations in the Middle East. Russia began a process of leap-frogging the Western powers, to alight amidst the Arab sheiks with a chest full of sumptuous delights which would fill the vacuum left by the departure of the Western competitor. Indeed, the foundation of the initial intrigues was the anti-Western mood of the newly independent countries. The refrain was, *We're enemies of your enemies, so why shouldn't we be friends?*

The master plan involved creating *dependence*, establishing *dominance*, then moving on to *annexation*. The first stage was the creation of a dependency in three distinct areas — military, economic, and political.

Military Dependence

Russian objectives become crystal clear with a casual rundown of the arms agreements consummated in the Middle East. Note the progression.

First Arms Deal	Country	Russia becomes Main or Exclusive Supplier
1955	Egypt	Main supplier
1955	Syria	Main supplier
1958	Iraq	Main supplier
1962	Algeria	Main supplier

1967	Sudan	Main supplier
1967	Yemen-South Yemen	Main supplier
1967	Iran (Terrorists)	Partial supplier
1970	Lybia	Partial supplier
1971	Lebanon (Terrorists)	Partial supplier

Items supplied to military arsenals included planes, tanks, artillery, missiles, naval vessels, electronic equipment, small arms, and sundry other materials.

It goes without saying that with the acceptance of military supplies, other elements enter. Replacements and parts come from the supplier and at his pleasure. Thus, military adventures must be sanctioned or at least tacitly supported. With supplies comes the need to import personnel to instruct, construct, and, in the case of the ultrasophisticated equipment, operators to man it. This accomplishes the most basic aim of all: *to establish a presence in the area marked for eventual occupation.* A further side benefit is the necessity of sending military and technical personnel to the Soviet Union for instruction — military and political.

By fostering the Arab-Israeli rift and doing all in her power to prolong the existing problem, Russia sees a golden opportunity to deepen Arab dependence and eventually find the opportunity to intervene as a benevolent protector.

Economic Dependence

Soviet economic programs have been initiated in Algeria, Egypt, Sudan, Yemen, South Yemen, Turkey, Syria, Iraq, and Iran. The amount of involvement varies significantly but generally follows a pattern in which projects initiated are long-term affairs allowing extended participation by the U.S.S.R. Examples of this may be seen in the Aswan Dam in Egypt (ten years) and the Euphrates Dam (eight to nine years). Hydroelectric projects have been initiated in Egypt,

Syria, Iraq, and Iran. Heavy and light industries, ports, roads and railways, irrigation projects, agriculture, fisheries, oil, natural gas, and numerous other offerings comprise the larder from which Arabs are encouraged to draw.

Syria and Egypt have become most heavily obligated to their Soviet mentors. Although accurate figures are not published, estimates claim that between 1954 and 1971 Egypt accepted some two billion in aid, while Syria's take was approximately $750,000,000 in economic assistance.

One of the prime areas of interest to the Soviets is the export-import alliances. Egypt provides an example of the pattern Russia would be delighted to establish throughout the area. Imports into Egypt from the Soviet Union stood at 1.5 percent in 1954. By 1970 the figure moved to 47 percent of all national imports. Exports kept pace. Forty and two-tenths percent of all export goods in 1970 were sent to the Soviet Union, while in 1954 the figure was only 1.4 percent.

It is of primary interest that the two countries in which Russia's most determined efforts are being expended are Israel's neighbors north and south.

Political Dependence

Russian contacts with Arab nations proceed without regard to how Communist parties happen to be faring in individual countries at any given time. Although there is no Arab Communist Party which operates legally, Communists with Russian orientation are known to be illegally active in Egypt, Syria, Sudan, South Yemen, Turkey, Iran, Jordan, Lebanon, and Iraq. In Algeria, Egypt, Syria, and Iraq, legitimate political organizations have had contact with the Soviet Communist Party.

Once again, Egypt provides a revealing view for examination. Here Russia attempted infiltration of the Arab Socialist Union in an effort to assure that leading individuals would be pro-Soviet in their allegiances. Interestingly enough, Moscow instructed the Egyptian Communist Party to voluntarily disband, and its members were instructed to join the Arab Socialist Union. They were then directed to seek key positions, with particular designs on the information media. In characteristically clandestine Russian operational fashion, secret groups were formed within the Socialist Union to create further mischief. The aim was to tie the knot with Russia much more securely. Anwar Sadat's purges in 1971, instigated to insure his control of Egyptian fortunes, seem to have decimated this movement. We may rest assured, however, that Russian determination and inventiveness being what it is, it is only a temporary arrest of momentum.

More productive, in a sense, is the creation of legitimate contacts between the Communist Party of Russia and the various political parties of the Arab states. These contacts allow Russian spokesmen to expose Communist ideas without running the risk of interfering with the internal affairs of the countries involved in the exchange of ideas. The Soviets attempt to impress the Arabs with their model, which they fondly hope will produce eventual union.

Tipping the Balance

While the foregoing are in process and the Soviets deftly tread the tightrope of détente and United Nations manipulation, the inflexible movement toward creating a military imbalance is the first priority. Comment has been made on the efficiency of the American Sixth Fleet's presence in thwarting Russia's high-handed attempts at expansion. It is no secret that the Soviet's long-sought naval superiority is viewed as one of the main ingredients in tipping the scale in her favor.

Since 1965 Russian naval presence in the Mediterranean has been a constant fixture. She has moved into the area vacated by the West and established bases from which to operate and duly impress locals with the strength of Soviet naval power. A concerted effort is being made to establish bases of operation throughout the area. Recently, Russia has requested permission from Spain to establish a permanent base on the Spanish coast. In Syria, Lattaqia welcomes the hammer and sickle. Far to the south, on the Indian Ocean, Aden and facilities on the island of Socotra serve as havens for seafaring comrades from the north.

There can be no mistaking Russian intentions in seeking global naval superiority. Some simple arithmetic will suffice.

	1960	1965	1970
Soviet nuclear submarines	3	35	70
Soviet guided-missile craft	10	57	170

Some will argue that the buildup of conventional weapons systems is simply an exercise in waste, in view of the nuclear capability of the superpowers. No nation, this reasoning supposes, would move into conventional warfare and run the risk of global holocaust. Three observations may be raised:

1. Russia apparently did just that during the Yom Kippur War. She rattled nuclear hardware in order to accomplish conventional objectives.

2. A nuclear deterrent serves just that purpose, to deter nuclear adventurism. Each adversary can assert decisively what can be delivered in the event one initiates conflagration. However, all pragmatic military thinking is done one step down — just below the nuclear threshold. Here conventional clout will dictate the terms and

determine victors and vanquished. Russia anticipates a final reaction, in view of catastrophic alternatives, in which the Middle East and the world will raise hands and say, "Better we be red than all of us dead."

3. According to the prophetic Scriptures, this is precisely what the Russian hordes will do when they decide to make a frontal military assault on the Middle East. Their move is seen as a conventional intrusion.

All of the historical background we have examined supports what the prophet predicted centuries ago and warns of the inevitability of its occurring.

A SHAKING IN THE LAND

At this point our attention, of necessity, must shift from the historical to the prophetical — which in actuality is history written before it is lived out. Ezekiel's precise account of the Russian invasion of the Middle East reads as a logical extension of the historical events and intents which we have scanned. The only missing factor seems to involve the element of timing — when will it happen? We, of course, cannot say with authority when it will take place. What can be observed with certainty is that the flow of events is even now moving in this direction.

A Clash of the Gods

Before we address ourselves to the examination of the details in Ezekiel 38-39 (each reader should carefully explore these chapters), it is imperative that some preliminary observations be made.

First, biblical prophetic scholars are convinced that the battle described in the passage before us is but the first in a campaign which will ultimately draw the armies of the nations to the Middle East. It must therefore be harmonized with Zechariah's prophecy and those compatible predictions presented to us in the New Testament. In our approach to the subject, it is not our intent to deal in a detailed manner with all issues of the era, only those major aspects which touch the prophetic history of the Chosen People.

It will be demonstrated that the momentum of interrelated events will bring human processes to a culmination — one which has not only been biblically predicted, but also has increasingly been the object of longing hearts and inquiring minds. Our faith must choose between one of two alternatives: a divine solution and His peace; or human schemes and catastrophe. Here we will present the biblical alternative.

Finally, we shall observe the distillation of hostilities to primary opponents, God and Satan. Before being tempted to dismiss this possibility as fanatical whimsy, let us pause and reflect for a moment. Those who refuse to accept the existence of a personal archfiend (a devil) need but ponder again the unreasoning antagonism unleashed on Israel over successive centuries. Simple deduction militates against any other realistic conclusion. The incision of psychopathic evil has torn too deeply into the fiber of human history to be swept away as a psychological mutant. History verifies what the Scriptures identify: Behind evil systems, which stand in defiant opposition to God, truth, and goodness, lurks the architect of moral and spiritual debauchery, Satan.

The ancient cry is raised: If this is true, why doesn't God, who is supposed to be in control of affairs among men and is deemed superior to any satanic character, do something? We can rest assured, *He is!* As the events of this chapter and the next unfold, we shall witness in prophetic foreview Jehovah's final solution to *Satan* and his *system*.

Russia presents the ultimate satanic system, atheistic Communism. The Western world will introduce the final impersonator of God, an Antichrist. He will represent in essence a personification of the satanic alternative to the biblical Messiah. God's response to these manifestations provides an intriguing and illuminating study.

My God, Your God

Nearly every war in human history has involved, at least in the minds of the respective opponents, more than mortal combatants. Nations take their gods to war with them; thus, god is pitted against god, and with the victory comes a triumph for the conqueror's deity. Of course, history is replete with cases in which this concept is made ludicrous by the fact that both contestants had less than honorable ends in view. Nonetheless, there are other illustrations in which good and evil were clearly in conflict. In these wars it could be said that the God of the universe and the god of this world were in direct confrontation — World War II can be cited as an unchallengeable example. So it has ever been. Whether in fact or fancy, clans, tribes, nations, and empires have appealed for their gods to empower mortals to win victories — mortals who could in turn place the garlands of their triumphs upon the altars of their respective deities. The process became an integral part, not only of the program of war, but of the pursuit of subsequent peace as well.

Aggressors move against those they hope to vanquish with three inescapable ends in view: *subjugation, humiliation, assimilation.*

Subjugation introduces the sequence. The design is to force the foe to capitulate — peacefully, if this can be accomplished, militarily if necessary.

Humiliation is the object of phase two. The aim is to instill in the conquered people a feeling of inferiority and defeat. In other words, they must come to accept being subjects. The ancients did this by insulting and carrying away gods or implements of worship venerated by the defeated people. In the process, they would defy these gods to do anything about it. Witness Rome's periodic desecration of the Jewish Temple and sacred Mount Moriah as evidence. Babylon did the same thing, as did Syria. The sequence is as old as history. It says, "Now you see, my god has defeated yours. Your god does not answer. You have been mastered."

Assimilation is the final objective in this process. After political ideologies and religious systems are dispossessed, the move is toward convincing the subjects to embrace the victor's system with its god. Of course, religion is the most emotional and unifying factor involved in true assimilation. If genuine religious union can be established — victor and vanquished join hands in worship at the same temple — then garrisoned troops can be sent home. Both the war and the victory have been won.

With the arrival of Communism came a system which is officially atheistic, and militantly so. It is the cumulative systematizing of all tyrannical tides that have risen over the centuries. Communism is the ultimate satanic device, having cast aside any pretense of lip service to a deity and blatantly declaring war on Almighty God. One wonders if we grasp the enormity of this phenomenon and all it implies. Thus, Communism sets itself apart as the uncompromising foe of every nation whose people own allegiance to any god, false or true. All dealings with any nation, such as the Arabs, declaring faith in a supreme being are seen as cynically condescending exercises pragmatically structured to gain an end. The long view is to subjugate both the people and their god. It can be no other way.

Russia's version of the succession described above is not to see nations joining hands in worship, but collectively raising the Soviet view — that is, *Paradise Found*, the final realization of the Marxist dream, the state supreme, the system triumphant. In this then, Communism is unique. It stands as the final manifestation of the evolution of satanically dominated political systems. Deposing Jehovah is the final stroke on the way to a new humanistic earth. In view of this, it is quite natural for Russia to spill her most noxious venom on the sons of Abraham. The three greatest religions known to man (Judaism, Christianity, and Islam) all sprang from Abraham's seed. Mastery of the Jew and his land would symbolize planting the banner of defiance on the totalitarian summit. From this perspective, the menacing designs of the Red Monster against little Israel take on overwhelmingly significant proportions.

I Will Call for a Sword

Russia's climactic intrusion into Israel is described by the prophet. Motivation for the venture is twofold:

> To take a spoil, and to take a prey; to turn thine hand upon the desolate places that are now inhabited, and upon the people that are gathered out of the nations, who have gotten cattle and goods, who dwell in the midst of the land (Ezek. 38:12).

One will notice that the invader comes *to take a spoil*. They also come "to turn thine hand...upon the people that are gathered out of the nations." Russian purposes are *exploitative*

— to possess the material wealth of the area and lay claim to the land. Exploitation is not the only driving force behind the assault, however. It is also *vindictive*. The hand of oppression is turned on the people. Daniel's account of the invasion (Dan. 11:36-45) reflects this element. The king of the north "shall go forth with great fury to destroy, and utterly to sweep many away" (Dan. 11:44). Anti-Semitic lust is seen once again lighting the passions of men. This time around, the divine response will be swift and sure. Daniel and Ezekiel agree regarding the fate awaiting the leader and his hosts. Daniel is specific: "yet he shall come to his end, and none shall help him" (Dan. 11:45). Ezekiel provides more detail:

> For in my jealousy and in the fire of my wrath have I spoken, Surely in that day there shall be a great shaking in the land of Israel...And I will call for a sword against him throughout all my mountains, saith the Lord GOD; every man's sword shall be against his brother. And I will enter into judgment against him with pestilence and with blood; and I will rain upon him, and upon his hordes, and upon the many people that are with him, an overflowing rain, and great hailstones, fire, and brimstone (Ezek. 38:19, 21-22).

Jehovah answers the salvos of the invader. Prominent throughout the account are repeated assertions of God's entry against the enemies of Israel. Great care is given to set forth precisely how this will take place. "I will call for a sword...saith the Lord GOD" (Ezek. 38:21). God's sword will be earthquake, pestilence, flood, hail, and lightning. Many believe this implies the use of nuclear devices to decimate the northern hosts. Perhaps so; but it does not seem to be the case. The Lord of creation, long defied and defamed by this blasphemous aggregation, will employ the elements they refused to believe He spoke into existence to seal their doom.

How often in history has this phenomenon been witnessed. Armies, which were unchallengeable by human force, were reduced to impotence before rain, snow, or disease. Grandiose schemes, carefully laid to raise new empires and subdue kingdoms, were swept into oblivion on the wings of the storm.

History remembers Sisera with 900 chariots of iron drawn up to do battle with Barak and his ill-equipped Israeli troops. "The stars in their courses fought against Sisera. The river of Kishon swept them away" (Jud. 5:20b-21a). A sudden storm turned what was ordinarily little more than a dry wash into an immobilizing torrent, before which an impregnable armored force was reduced to a motley group of retreating fugitives.

Sennacherib of Assyria bawled his threats before besieged Jerusalem. "Let not thy God, in whom thou trustest, deceive thee" (Isa. 37:10). Isaiah the prophet serenely delivered the divine reply. "He shall not come into this city, nor shoot an arrow there...For I [Jehovah] will defend this city, to save it, for mine own sake, and for my servant David's sake" (2 Ki. 19:32, 34). The next morning, anxious Jews were startled to see no smoke from cooking fires over the Assyrian encampment, only a pall of death. One hundred eighty-five thousand corpses littered the landscape. "The angel of the LORD went out, and smote in the camp of the Assyrians an hundred fourscore and five thousand" (2 Ki. 19:35). Herodotus, the Roman historian, says, "A multitude of field mice by night devoured all the quivers and bows of the enemy, and all the straps by which they held their shields." Consequently, they were left defenseless. The story cannot be substantiated, but think of the irony in it: Sennacherib's unstoppable army brought low by divinely dispatched mice! Whatever the means, the result is history.

Myths of Napoleonic invincibility died amidst the swirling blizzards in Russia. The snows accomplished what the armies of Europe could not. Bonaparte's dream of a grand empire was cast into irreversible decline by the weather.

Yet once more this will be the case — and here the most devastating demonstration man has witnessed. The northern invaders will be inundated by the storm, pierced by the lightning shaft, and battered to earth by decapitating hailstones. Over it all rings the solemn word: "I will call for a sword...." Russia will learn what we all must, that no man or nation can defy omnipotence with immunity!

> Thou shalt fall upon the mountains of Israel,
> thou, and all thy hordes, and the peoples that
> are with thee; I will give thee unto the
> ravenous birds of every sort, and to the beasts
> of the field to be devoured (Ezek. 39:4).

Dazed remnants will retreat to the north — all but one-sixth of the force will be destroyed — while carrion birds go silently about their business.

How sure can we be that this will happen? Remember the certainty of fulfillment which we have seen to this point. Then consider the words, "Thou shalt fall upon the open field; *for I have spoken it, saith the Lord GOD*" (Ezek. 39:5). How sure is it? As sure as the Word of God.

> "I will call for a sword," Jehovah has said,
> And leave the Red hordes to number their dead.
> To strike with a shaking, the flood, and great hail,
> My spear gleaming lightning to pierce through their mail.
> Dread silence will reign on the face of the land,
> All ears fallen deaf to the sound of command.
> Now frozen in death hands that wielded the sword,

Brought low in the end by the voice of the Lord.
So birds wing their way where once raged the strife,
To light midst the shambles, bereft of all life.
Behold, it is done, and let it be known,
The arm of Jehovah was bared for His own.
                                                    E. McQ.

Why all of this? Ezekiel gives us the answer: "Thus will I magnify myself, and sanctify myself; and I will be known in the eyes of many nations, and they shall know that I am the LORD" (Ezek. 38:23).

By the close of the sequence of events engulfing the planet in the "end time," all men, Jew and Gentile alike, will know that I am the Lord.

Thy King cometh unto thee....

CHAPTER TEN

TRAUMA AND TRIUMPH

A T THIS POINT we begin our consideration of aspects which are more exclusively prophetic in nature. Before we undertake this, it will be helpful to look back at the central features in God's plan for His people, Israel.

Dispersion, preservation, and *restoration* comprise the time line along which the nation has moved through history to this point. It is as unmistakable as it is compellingly fascinating. Before us is a people divinely set apart to be a peculiar demonstration of the bedrock propositions set forth in the Bible. Through the entire process we are allowed to view parallel manifestations: man at his worst, and God in His faithfulness.

Man at His Worst

Gentile treatment of the Chosen People across the long centuries of suffering will forever do away with the fiction that man in his present state is naturally good and left to his native proclivities will soar to divine heights. It simply is not true. Witnessing the fact that today Israel is surrounded by millions of people who cry for her annihilation give credence to the somber assertion that there has been no moral evolution cycling in the human breast. Moderns are as capableof cruelty, suppression, and purely self-serving tactics as were their ancient counterparts.

Of course, this sad disclosure is already patently evident to all realistic people. However, it needs to be restated in order for us to grasp something which seems to escape us frequently. It is precisely at this point that human fantasy and biblical reality part ways. Many profess to be repelled by the final convulsive monstrosities of human behavior revealed in the Bible, to the point of scoffing at the apocalyptic portions of Scripture. The fact is, man is quite capable of committing the horrendous acts described in the sacred accounts. He has the weapons at hand. And, there are certainly at any point in history men available who, given the opportunity, will do anything which will hold the promise of placing them on top of the heap when the dust of the holocaust settles. Credit the Bible with what can always be said of it: It has always told it like it was and would be — no wishful illusions, just man as he is.

God allows us to look into the process before it occurs. While this is true, we must be aware of the fact that Jehovah, although being fully cognizant of the facts of the future, is not the perpetrator of man's belligerence. Man is a fallen creature. God is no more the author of his infamous acts than He was of the original fall. He is simply allowing us to see man at his worst and, in so doing, allow us to anticipate the future and prepare for it.

God in His Faithfulness

Through all of the events recorded in the pages before us shines one grand design: the reconciliation and establishment of Israel in the glory Jehovah promised through the prophetic Word. While we are allowed to see man at his worst, we are also afforded a preview of the great purposes of God for His people.

We must bear in mind that we are involved in eternal processes. Our time-shaded perspective of history is as a speck of dust on a horizon that is as broad as the life span of God himself. From the divine point of view, we are moving through an orderly sequence of events which will, in the end, bring us to the culminating terminal where all things promised find fruition.

At the outset of our consideration, we should see two passages which delineate God's unalterable attitude toward His people. The first comes to us through the Pharisee turned Apostle of Christ, Paul. Jeremiah the prophet brings the next word, which illustrates the message of both the Old and New Testaments regarding Israel.

> I say, then, Hath God cast away His people? God forbid...And so all Israel shall be saved; as it is written, There shall come out of Zion the Deliverer, and shall turn away ungodliness from Jacob (Rom. 11:1, 26).

> And they shall be my people, and I will be their God; And I will give them one heart, and one way, that they may fear me forever, for the good of them, and their children after them (Jer. 32:38-39).

Fulfillment of God's program will come in three distinct phases: *breaking the Gentile sword; the revelation of Messiah; the reconciliation and establishment of Israel.*

BREAKING THE GENTILE SWORD

Russian Communism is but one manifestation of Gentile intransigence in the face of Jehovah's right to reign over the affairs of men. The entire flow of the history of Gentile world powers has been cast in a similar mold. The Prophet Daniel provides a striking overview of nations as they are viewed from horizontal and vertical perspectives.

From the human level, successive world empires are seen in the form of a colossal figure. King Nebuchadnezzar of Babylon dreamed his dream of a "great image...whose brightness was excellent...and the form of it was terrible" (Dan. 2:31). In his vision he saw the coming empires pictured as gold, silver, bronze, and iron entities which joined to form this spectacular statue. The principal contingents represented in the image were later identified as Babylon, Medo-Persia, Greece, and a Roman system which would have ancient and modern counterparts. To say the least, it was impressive to human eyes — awe-inspiring might be nearer the mark. So much so, that the king built a huge replica of gold and set it up in the plain of Dura as a proper representation of his royal properties. He required his subjects to bow down and worship the monument or die. Thus the famous confrontation with the three Hebrew children and their brief stay within the confines of the "fiery furnace" (Dan. 3).

The episode is reflective of the folly recurrent in Gentile history: seeing the state, both the system and potentate, as objects worthy of veneration, while the worship of Jehovah is displaced. The empire stands in God's place and demands total loyalty. Often this allegiance takes the form of worshiping the gods that have been created by the nations themselves. The point is, whether men bow to an emperor, a man-made god, or a humanistic philosophy, the result is the same. God is out of His place in the heart of man, and man is out of his place in the program of God.

Even in the representation of the great image, which man persistently views from his own whimsy, the divine finger pens the final result. God states that there will be, not four empires, but five.

> And in the days of these kings shall the God
> of heaven set up a kingdom, which shall never
> be destroyed; and the kingdom shall not be
> left to other people, but it shall break in pieces

and consume all these kingdoms, and it shall stand forever (Dan. 2:44).

With this declaration, Jehovah injects the concept of a coming divine kingdom through which He will order affairs upon the scene of human events.

From the up-to-down view, God gave His Prophet Daniel heaven's evaluation of what the King of Babylon saw.

Daniel spoke and said, I saw in my vision by night, and, behold, the four winds of heaven strove upon the great sea. And four great beasts came up from the sea, diverse one from another (Dan. 7:2-3).

These same empires are seen as voracious animals, preying upon one another — stalking, crushing, devouring those who were weaker than they. The inflexible rule of force was the dominant characteristic of these imperial marauders. And so it has been; the strong survive while the weak are consumed and subjugated. Within the framework of this scheme of things, only two considerations seem valid: first, to have the strength to dominate, or at least fend off enemies; second, to possess the will to employ that force when national interests are at stake. Any other approach to the might-is-right posture of world systems will very likely prove fatal for the indulgents.

Once again, at the very heart of the revelation, God lays bare His eventual response to man's cherished alternatives to Jehovah's sovereign rule.

I beheld till the thrones were placed, and the Ancient of days did sit...I saw in the night visions, and, behold, one like the Son of man came with the clouds of heaven, and came to the Ancient of days, and they brought him near before him. And there was given him dominion,

and glory, and a kingdom, that all people,
nations, and languages should serve him; his
dominion is an everlasting dominion, which
shall not pass away, and his kingdom that which
shall not be destroyed (Dan. 7:9a, 13-14).

The Bible clearly asserts that before the Messiah's kingdom
reign is established, Gentile powers will be finally and
emphatically broken.

Kings' Row

Scripture affords us a fascinating foreview of the combines
of national alliances which will hold sway in the latter phases
of this segment of history. These alliances congregate under
figures who hold greater or lesser degrees of notoriety in the
biblical accounts.

The King of the North

Daniel uses this appellation (Dan. 11:40) to describe the
leader of Russia and his hostile confederacy. Included in the
roster of nations outlined in the chapters we have already
considered (Ezek. 38-39) are those from the North, Europe,
the Middle East, and Africa. They will follow their leader into
the resounding defeat described in the preceding chapter.

The King of the South

He is also mentioned by Daniel (Dan. 11:40) and associated
with the invasion of Israel. Apparently, this king initially
moves in league with the King of the North, only to be
betrayed and overrun. Historically this leader has been
identified as the ruler of Egypt. He will consort with and
represent those North African and Arab states who join the
southern grouping. Prophetic scholars viewed with interest
the efforts of Anwar Sadat to establish a role as the dominant
leader in the Arab world.

The Kings of the East

Revelation 16:12 tells of a coalition of kings from beyond the Euphrates who will be involved in the final struggles. These representatives are conceded to be the powers of the Far East. Another passage in the Revelation (9:16) gives the number of this invading horde as two hundred million troops. It is significant to note that Red China is reported to have declared recently she is now capable of fielding a land army approximating these figures!

The Western Leader

The most sinister of all of these end-time personalities is the leader of the Western nations. He is held by most prophetic scholars, on authority of Daniel 7 and other texts, to be the leader of a form of the revived Roman system — a confederation of states within the boundaries of the Old Roman Empire. Some believe that the geographical extent may even exceed those under the sway of ancient Rome.

He is called by various names in Scripture. The Beast, The Man of Sin, and the Willful King are three of the designations by which he is identified. The most prominent title ascribed to him is Antichrist. It is perhaps the description most consistent with his total character; for he is seen entering the Temple in Jerusalem, placing an image there, announcing himself to be God, and demanding universal worship (2 Th. 2:3-4).

In these alliances we view the final form of Gentile power, powers which will be active in the last days. The sobering thing to note is that they are, at this moment, roughly aligned in the relative positions outlined in the Bible.

A Gathering in the Land

Both Testaments verify an assembling of the nations in the Middle East for one climactic confrontation. Proportionately, mankind has not witnessed anything remotely akin to what the bible enunciates for this period. Christ referred to it as a time of "great tribulation, such as was not since the beginning of the world to this time, no, nor ever shall be" (Mt. 24:21). Jeremiah spoke of it as "the time of Jacob's trouble" (Jer. 30:7).

The Scriptures universally agree that the period will see the nations of the world come together to do battle, with Israel once again in the middle of the fray. Joel put it this way:

> Proclaim this among the nations, Prepare war, wake up the mighty men, let all the men of war draw near; let them come up; Beat your plowshares into swords, and your pruning hooks into spears; let the weak say, I am strong. Assemble yourselves, and come, all ye nations, and gather yourselves together round about; there cause thy mighty ones to come down, O LORD (Joel 3:9-11).

Zechariah took up the theme:

> Behold, the day of the LORD cometh, and thy spoil shall be divided in the midst of thee. For I will gather all nations against Jerusalem to battle...I will make Jerusalem a cup of trembling unto all the peoples round about, when they shall be in the siege both against Judah and against Jerusalem. And in that day will I make Jerusalem a burdensome stone for all peoples; all that burden themselves with it shall be cut in pieces, though all the nations of the earth be gathered together against it (Zech. 14:1-2a; 12:2-3).

John the apostle voiced agreement through his description:

> ...go forth unto the kings of the earth and of the whole world, to gather them to the battle

> of that great day of God Almighty...And he
> gathered them together into a place called
> in the Hebrew tongue Armageddon (Rev.
> 16:14, 16).

Israel will be beset by menacing forces that will come into the land to initiate a campaign which will, for a time, run the length and breadth of the region.

The intensity of the struggles of this brief period, described so vividly by the Prophet Daniel and the Apostle John, are unmatched in human history. Christ, in response to a specific question by his disciples regarding the last days, stated,

> For then shall be great tribulation, such as was
> not since the beginning of the world to this
> time, no, nor ever shall be. And except those
> days should be shortened, there should no flesh
> be saved; but for the elect's sake those days
> shall be shortened (Mt. 24:21-22).

This statement grips the essence of the period as it is expressed everywhere in Scripture. Tribulation dominates the world scene. It is born by acts of satanically emboldened men on the one hand and Jehovah on the other. While the nations clamor and maneuver to dominate international affairs, God moves in with cataclysmic judgments upon mankind. A succession of calamities, divinely sent, buffet the population of the globe. It is unmistakably evident that they will be initiated by man's Maker. Yet, rather than repent and acknowledge God, men persist in defying Him. "And blasphemed the name of God, who hath power over these plagues; and they repented not to give him glory" (Rev. 16:9).

These awful days will be marked by suffering, warfare, and defiance of God. Suffering will be perpetrated through pestilence, famine, and persecution. Once again, the heel of oppression will fall on the Jewish people. This time hostility will also fall heavily upon those who dare to own allegiance to Jesus Christ. The blood of those who acknowledge Christ as Savior will wet the tyrant's sword.

As was stated earlier, following an extended period of international unrest, warfare will settle in the Middle East. Israel will be marked out as the primary recipient of Gentile virulence.

Finally, the aforementioned Antichrist will officially personify the dreadful character typified by Antiochus Epiphanes in his infamous desecration of the Temple in bygone days. Scripture describes this "abomination of desolation" foretold by Daniel and Jesus Christ (Dan. 12:11; Mt. 24:15). It is viewed as the consummate act of man's rebellious pilgrimage on this planet (2 Th. 2:4; Rev. 13).

So it is that humanity gathers for its Armageddon. All historical byways have directed man's pathway steadily toward it. Gentile nations will stand poised, in their view, to annihilate Israel and forever depose Jehovah. Jewry will turn eyes heavenward to face the Messiah.

REVELATION OF MESSIAH

Much earlier in this work, a Jewish historian was quoted who pointed out the fact that in times of great national distress, Jewish people long for the homeland and yearn for the coming Messiah. This phenomenon coincides with the sequence outlined in both Testaments. When the final trauma is mentioned, it is inevitably followed by a passage depicting the coming triumph of the Messiah. A few examples will demonstrate.

Joel's Word

The Prophet Joel set forth the sequence in his word to us. We read,

> Proclaim this among the nations, Prepare war, wake up the mighty men, let all the men of war draw near; let them come up. Beat your

> plowshares into swords, and your pruning
> hooks into spears; let the weak say, I am strong.
> Assemble yourselves, and come, all ye nations,
> and gather yourselves together round about;
> there cause thy mighty ones to come down,
> O LORD (Joel 3:9-11).

The next few verses take up the theme of the ensuing judgment which will come upon the nations as a result of this gathering. Following this, Joel stated: "The LORD also shall roar out of Zion, and utter his voice from Jerusalem, and the heavens and the earth shall shake; but the LORD will be the hope of his people, and the strength of the children of Israel" (Joel 3:16). Restoration and the reign of the Messiah and His people fill out the narrative.

Zechariah's Comment

Zechariah further clarified the matter with his detailed chronicle of events surrounding Messiah's intervention.

> Behold, the day of the LORD cometh, and thy
> spoil shall be divided in the midst of thee. For
> I will gather all nations against Jerusalem to
> battle...Then shall the LORD go forth, and fight
> against those nations, as when he fought in
> the day of battle. And his feet shall stand in
> that day upon the Mount of Olives, which is
> before Jerusalem on the east...and the LORD,
> my God, shall come, and all the saints with
> thee (Zech. 14:1-5).

Once again the inspired writer moved on to expound the establishment and quality of the kingdom rule of the reigning Messiah. Central to the passage are these words: "And the LORD shall be king over all the earth; in that day there shall be one LORD, and his name one" (Zech. 14:9).

Jesus Agrees

Christ followed the sequence. He described the rigors of the time of tribulation which will precede Messiah's coming, then said,

> Immediately after the tribulation of those days shall the sun be darkened, and the moon shall not give its light, and the stars shall fall from heaven, and the powers of the heavens shall be shaken. And then shall appear the sign of the Son of man in heaven; and then shall all the tribes of the earth mourn, and they shall see the Son of man coming in the clouds of heaven with power and great glory (Mt. 24:29-30).

Jesus went on to describe the establishment of the messianic reign. He prefaced these words with this statement: "And he shall send his angels with a great sound of a trumpet, and they shall gather together his elect from the four winds, from one end of heaven to the other" (Mt. 24:31).

Paul's Witness

Paul picked up the refrain in his message to the Thessalonians. He was responding to their query about the "day of the Lord." His reply makes note of the entrance and foul work of the "man of sin," the Antichrist whose actions will dominate the troubled closing days of this age. He went on to assure them, "And then shall that wicked one be revealed, whom the Lord shall consume with the spirit of his mouth, and shall destroy with the brightness of his coming" (2 Th. 2:8).

In conjunction with this thought, the apostle referred to the total restoration of Israel following the Lord's coming. This is recorded in the Epistle to the Romans in a passage previously mentioned.

John's Perspective

After he described the dark days of the time of Tribulation with its thunderous judgments, manic tyrants, and suffering saints, John lit the sky with an awesome description of the coming of the Messiah to set things right.

> And I saw the heaven opened and, behold, a white horse; and he that sat upon him was called Faithful and True, and in righteousness he doth judge and make war. His eyes were like a flame of fire, and on his head were many crowns; and he had a name written, that no man knew, but he himself. And he was clothed with a vesture dipped in blood; and his name is called The Word of God. And the armies that were in heaven followed him upon white horses, clothed in fine linen, white and clean. And out of his mouth goeth a sharp sword, that with it he should smite the nations, and he shall rule them with a rod of iron; and he treadeth the winepress of the fierceness and wrath of Almighty God. And he hath on his vesture and on his thigh a name written, KING OF KINGS, AND LORD OF LORDS (Rev. 19:11-16).

He then gave us sublime words about the kingdom age under the Messiah's sovereignty. Still the sequence holds true — *tribulation, revelation,* and *restoration.*

It should be noted that the Messiah's appearance will not be the result of man's ability to create conditions which will be conducive to the entrance of a divine King. In other words, no religious, political, or philosophical system will be triumphant to the point of preparing the way for the Messiah. In fact, the exact reverse will be true. Spiritual, moral, and political conditions will deteriorate until mankind is brought to the brink of the global conflagration so long feared by members of the world community.

Equally noteworthy is the fact that this is what the Bible has always said, even through times of euphoric optimism in which man saw the approach of a golden age through science, education, and technology. From our current vantage point, we have a more realistic view of the calamities which await Adam's sons.

In scanning the whole of the Bible on the subject, there can be no doubt that the Messiah is set forth as One who will make a spectacular personal appearance at a future point in history. Attempts to assign the messianic passages to the nation Israel, a phantom ideal, or any other proffered consideration will simply not square with the clear message of the holy Scriptures. Nor will any other proposition meet the universal human need that only the King of glory can satisfy.

For Bible believers, Jews and Gentiles, the issue does not really settle on if or what He will be but actually who He is. The identity of the Messiah is the taproot of the division between evangelical believers and Jewish people who acknowledge the authority of Scriptures. On the surface, this statement may seem to be extremely simplistic. The truth is, it is one that is all too often obscured in the heat of peripheral questions. It is the fundamental consideration which all men, Jews and Gentiles, must honestly face.

The Messiah's Identity

Who is the King of Israel? How can we recognize Him? These are the two most basic questions faced by Jews and Gentiles — essential not simply because of their national and international application but because they are indispensable to our personal relationship to God.

Old Testament messianic Scriptures set forth two precise views of the work of the predicted Deliverer: *sufferer* and *sovereign*. Four dominant alternatives grew out of the accepted interpretations of the concept.

1. A belief in the appearance of the two Messiahs.
2. The sufferer would not be a personality but, rather, the nation Israel in her persecutions.
3. Choose the most desirable manifestation and reject the other.
4. Accept the revelation as depicting one Messiah in two appearances.

A Composite of the Messiah as Sufferer

The keynote comes with Zechariah's word concerning the coming King.

> Rejoice greatly, O daughter of Zion; shout, O daughter of Jerusalem; behold, thy King cometh unto thee; he is just, and having salvation; lowly, and riding upon an ass, and upon a colt, the foal of an ass (Zech. 9:9).

Three notes are struck here. The King *comes*; He comes in *humility*; He brings *salvation*. Around these distinct considerations, God draws His purposes in the Messiah's ministry of suffering.

This King would be betrayed into the hands of His oppressors: "Yea, mine own familiar friend, in whom I trusted, who did eat of my bread, hath lifted up his heel against me" (Ps. 41:9).

Psalm 22 is the first of the great trilogy which portrays the full-orbed ministry of the Messiah as suffering Savior, ministering Shepherd, and reigning Monarch. His suffering is described in startling details.

> My God, my God, why hast thou forsaken me?...But I am a worm, and no man; a reproach of men, and despised by the people. All they

> who see me laugh me to scorn; they shoot
> out the lip, they shake the head, saying, He
> trusted on the LORD that he would deliver
> him; let him deliver him, seeing he delighteth
> in him...I am poured out like water, and all
> my bones are out of joint...my tongue cleaveth
> to my jaws; and thou hast brought me into
> the dust of death...they pierced my hands and
> my feet...They part my garments among them,
> and cast lots upon my vesture (Ps. 22:1, 6-8,
> 14-16, 18).

The psalm abruptly turns from suffering and death to
resurrection and victory for the Sufferer and the sons of
Jacob:

> I will declare thy name unto my brethren; in
> the midst of the congregation will I praise thee.
> Ye who fear the LORD, praise him; all ye, the
> seed of Jacob, glorify him; and fear him, all ye,
> the seed of Israel. For he hath not despised nor
> abhorred the affliction of the afflicted, neither
> hath he hidden his face from him; but when
> he cried unto him, he heard (Ps. 22:22-24).

Isaiah joined David at the easel to complete the portrait.

> He is despised and rejected of men, a man of
> sorrows, and acquainted with grief, and we hid
> as it were our faces from him; he was despised,
> and we esteemed him not. Surely he hath borne
> our griefs, and carried our sorrows; yet we did
> esteem him stricken, smitten of God, and
> afflicted. But he was wounded for our trans-
> gressions, he was bruised for our iniquities; the
> chastisement for our peace was upon him, and
> with his stripes we are healed. All we like sheep

have gone astray; we have turned every one
to his own way, and the LORD hath laid on
him the iniquity of us all. He was oppressed,
and he was afflicted, yet he opened not his
mouth; he is brought as a lamb to the slaughter,
and as a sheep before her shearers is dumb,
so he openeth not his mouth...For he was cut
off out of the land of the living; for the
transgression of my people was he stricken...Yet
it pleased to LORD to bruise him; he hath put
him to grief. When thou shalt make his soul
an offering for sin...He shall see the travail of
his soul, and shall be satisfied; by his knowledge
shall my righteous servant justify many; for he
shall bear their iniquities (Isa. 53:3-8, 10-11).

As was true in David's declaration, Isaiah moved from the
trauma of suffering to the glories of the Messiah's triumph.

Therefore will I divide him a portion with the
great, and he shall divide the spoil with the
strong, because he hath poured out his soul
unto death; and he was numbered with the
transgressors; and he bore the sin of many,
and made intercession for the transgressors
(Isa. 53:12).

On the basis of this justification, Israel is instructed to
"break forth into singing, and cry aloud...Enlarge the place
of thy tent...and thy seed shall inherit the nations...Fear
not...For thy Maker is thine husband; the LORD of hosts is
his name; and thy Redeemer, the Holy One of Israel; The
God of the whole earth shall he be called" (Isa. 54:1-5).

Again, sequentially, the Messiah's sovereign reign — which
we will view shortly — follows His suffering. There is very
good reason for God's initiating this progression.

Fit Subjects for the King

The kingdom of God, we know, will have a fit King. The suffering of the Messiah would assure a basis on which we might become *fit subjects*. There could be no true kingdom until the hearts of the subjects were of one accord with Jehovah. This could only be fully accomplished by a program of propitiatory reconciliation which is beyond the ability of humans to culminate. In other words, if man were to be saved, it would be God who would do the saving.

Israel's entire system of worship reflected this. After earnest Israelites had done their best to abide by the stern strictures of the laws and commandments, they came with their sacrifices to petition God for mercy. Why? They were, on the one hand, obeying the command of God to do so. Yet, they were also people who recognized that for all of their doing, they were failures still. They were sinners still and stood in need of a Redeemer — a Savior. The sacrifice was God's answer to man's need. In the suffering of the Messiah, Jehovah erected His antitypical sacrificial altar and there forever met the demands of divine justice. Once and for all He provided for man's need. All that smoldering altars and ministering priests reflected of the yearning of petitioners for full justification was delivered. The Lord *bruised Him* that through *His stripes* we could be healed as *the Lord laid on him the iniquity of us all.*

Only one man in all of the annals of mankind has presented proper credentials as the suffering Messiah. He is a Jew; a Jew who longed for the redemption of Israel as none ever had; a Jew who said and did what no human being ever approached in word or deed; a Jew who, by any standard of measurement, towers above all religious teachers, military men, politicians, philosophers, or educators ever to step upon the stage of human history; a Jew who, when left off the list of the "Ten Greatest Men in History" compiled by a world figure, would receive the supreme accolade, "Oh I did not include Jesus Christ because He is in a class by Himself, He is incomparable."

Jesus Christ was a Jew who predicted His death for sinful humanity, and He then willingly went to it. Jesus Christ was a Jew who said He would triumph over death and vacate a tomb, and He did it. Jesus Christ was a Jew who offered Himself as the Savior of all, Jew and Gentile, who would receive Him and has demonstrated over the centuries in the lives of believers that He is all He claims to be. Jesus Christ was a Jew who predicted what the world would ultimately come to, and we are witnessing the truth of His words. Jesus Christ was a Jew who promised to return to His chosen people as a reconciling and reigning Messiah, and He soon shall. Jesus Christ was a Jew who declared that His kingdom would one day cover the earth, "as the waters cover the sea," with justice, righteousness, and peace — we yearn for that day to come!

Why Didn't Israel's Leadership Accept Him?

Probably for the same reasons most people alive today do not, namely *pride, power,* and *preference.*

Jesus Christ told them they would have to acknowledge being sinners, just like the rest of us. They could not abide that. It was simply more than their religious pride could take. To reduce a proud Pharisee to the plane of ordinary people who needed saving was unthinkable to them. Put the same requirement to the majority of people today who profess themselves to be religious, and measure their reactions. The result will likely be the same.

Jesus taught His hearers that power with God was to be found in serving and ministering, not in being lords over the people. He spoke of bearing crosses and becoming servants, taking the lowly place and being deferential in treatment of others. Religious leaders reacted negatively to those propositions. The truth is, they almost always do. This was not a Jewish problem but a human one. Had Christ promised a system which would have delivered power into their hands, they would no doubt have been happy to receive Him. But as history has demonstrated, religious power without the tempering humility Christ demanded can become a withering instrument of oppression. Of all people on the earth, Jews have witnessed this in the plagues brought upon them by their *religious* Gentile tormentors.

Finally, given a choice between a sufferer and a triumphant King, they opted for what they preferred — someone who would promise to handle the Roman tyrant. They had had enough of suffering and humiliation. They wanted to hear promises of grandeur and glory. Even Christ's disciples were not immune to this. Persistently they pressed for the establishment of the kingdom immediately and were stunned when He predicted His death and suffering at the hands of their enemies. Actually, they were seeing only what they chose to see in the prophetic Scriptures.

This is not to infer that all people in the religious systems contemporary with Christ were corrupt individuals. This was certainly not the case, as many were sincere worshipers of Jehovah. However, as is often true, those of a less spiritual turn of mind had labored successfully to grasp the reins of power.

Christ was so totally nonpartisan religiously and politically that, in the end, all parties would conspire to destroy Him. His consistent refusal to manipulate or be manipulated was beyond the ken of self-serving interest groups. The rule of God was His obsession; their success was theirs.

RECONCILIATION AND
ESTABLISHMENT OF ISRAEL

No more glorious strain runs through the Scriptures than the revelation of the full establishment of the kingdom of the Messiah. Zechariah marked the inception of this fulfilling period as the time when "I will pour upon the house of David, and upon the inhabitants of Jerusalem, the Spirit of grace and of supplications; and they shall look upon me whom they have pierced, and they shall mourn for him, as one mourneth for his only son, and shall be in bitterness for him, as one that is in bitterness for his firstborn" (Zech. 12:10).

> When all our friends deserted,
> > While vicious foes assailed,
> We looked for consolation,
> > But every means had failed.
>
> Our eyes now search the heavens,
> > Red-rimmed with bitter shame,
> At our long-time refusal
> > To call Messiah's name.
>
> Then rend these war-soiled garments,
> > Our cry before Him rings:
> "Come Savior-Christ, Deliver!"
> > Behold, the KING OF KINGS.
> > > E. McQ.

The mourning of embattled Israel is answered by the appearance of the once "pierced" Messiah-Savior. "And his feet shall stand in that day upon the Mount of Olives, which is before Jerusalem on the east, and the Mount of Olives shall cleave in its midst toward the east and toward the west, and there shall be a very great valley...and the LORD, my God, shall come, and all the saints with thee" (Zech. 14:4-5).

Joel identified this great valley which will be opened at the Messiah's return as the place where the nations will be brought for judgment.

> I will also gather all nations, and will bring them
> down into the Valley of Jehoshaphat, and will

judge them there for my people and for my heritage, Israel, whom they have scattered among the nations, and parted my land. And they have cast lots for my people, and have given a boy for an harlot, and sold a girl for wine, that they might drink (Joel 3:2-3).

When one stands upon the Mount of Olives and looks across the Kidron Valley toward the walls of the Old City, he sees mute witness of the major religions' affirmation of faith in these words. Moslems, Christians, and Jews have all established cemeteries there in anticipation of a future judgment.

The Least of These My Brethren

Jesus Christ made an arresting declaration in His statement about this event. It is a word which falls into perfect harmony with what has been outlined by the above quotations.

When the Son of man shall come in his glory, and all the holy angels with him, then shall he sit upon the throne of his glory. And before him shall be gathered all the nations; and he shall separate them one from another, as a shepherd divideth his sheep from the goats...Then shall the King say unto them on his right hand, Come, ye blessed of my Father, inherit the kingdom prepared for you from the foundation of the world; For I was hungry, and ye gave me food; I was thirsty, and ye gave me drink; I was a stranger, and ye took me in; Naked, and ye clothed me; I was sick, and ye visited me; I was in prison, and ye came unto me (Mt. 25:31-32, 34-36).

The righteous raise the query, "when saw we thee hungry...or thirsty...a stranger...or naked...sick or in prison...?" (Mt. 25:37-39). The King replies, "Verily I say unto you, Inasmuch as ye have done it unto *one of the least of these my brethren*, ye have done it unto me" (Mt. 25:40). Who are the "least of these my brethren" referred to here? There is no doubt, they are the sons of Abraham — Israel.

Jesus agreed with the words of Joel that the basis for the judgment of the Gentile nations preceding the kingdom period will be "for my people and for my heritage, Israel, whom they have scattered among the nations, and parted my land" (Joel 3:2).

Jehovah's word to Abraham, therefore, rings clearer still: "I will bless them that bless thee, and curse him that curseth thee" (Gen. 12:3). In a very real sense, the Scriptures, Old Testament and New, tell us that he who raises a hand against the Jewish people, even through the long night of the Dispersion, raises a hand against God and can expect to be fully requited for his arrogance. So the anguished Jewish cry of the centuries is answered. Justice will be served. Our God has assured us of this.

Following the encounter in the Vale of Jehosphaphat, "the LORD shall be king over all the earth; in that day shall there be one LORD, and his name one" (Zech. 14:9). Thus will be ushered in the age when all of the biblical declarations predicting Israel's full restoration and reestablishment will be fully realized. It will be the day of the final Aliyah: *the Ascenders will have reached the summit.*

Reconciliation

Jeremiah anticipated this when he said,

> But this shall be the covenant that I will make with the house of Israel: After those days, saith the LORD, I will put my law in their inward parts, and write it in their hearts, and will be their God, and they shall be my people. And they shall teach no more every man his neigh-

> bor, and every man his brother, saying, Know
> the LORD; for they shall all know me, from
> the least of them unto the greatest of them,
> saith the LORD; for I will forgive their iniquity,
> and I will remember their sin no more (Jer.
> 31:33-34).

This is what Paul had in mind when he wrote, "all Israel
shall be saved" (Rom. 11:26). All of the Jews of the period
will know the Lord. The nation will become a theocracy
in the ultimate sense of the term. It will be a day when
Jew and redeemed Gentile will join hands to unite under
the banner of the reigning Messiah-Savior. Ancient
animosities will be forever put away. Spiritual union, with
the "middle wall of partition" fully broken down, will be
the order of the day.

Regathering

Moses, Isaiah, Ezekiel, and Jeremiah joined the chorus of
prophetic heralds who confidently intoned the regathering
and full resurgence of the scattered nation. This illustrious
quartet offered superb harmony in their predictive melodies
of the certainty of the final return.

Moses: "That then the LORD thy God will turn thy captivity,
and have compassion upon thee, and will return and gather
thee from all the nations where the LORD thy God hath
scattered thee" (Dt. 30:3).

Isaiah: "Fear not; for I am with thee. I will bring thy seed
from the east, and gather thee from the west. I will say to
the north, Give up; and to the south, Keep not back; bring
my sons from far, and my daughters from the ends of the
earth" (Isa. 45:5-6).

Jeremiah: "Behold, I will send for many fishers, saith the LORD,
and they shall fish them; and afterward will I send for many
hunters, and they shall hunt them from every mountain, and
from every hill, and out of the clefts of the rocks" (Jer. 16:16).

Ezekiel: "Therefore, thus said the Lord GOD: Now will I bring again the captivity of Jacob, and have mercy upon the whole house of Israel, and will be jealous for my holy name" (Ezek. 39:25).

Today Zionists, Jews, and Christians alike recognize the validity of the rights of the Jewish people to a national homeland in the Middle East. In this yet future day, the full scope of that right will be realized.

Reestablishment

The Messiah's throne will be established in an Israel which will occupy the expansive geographical area promised to the Patriarch Abraham. All current territorial arguments are only academic sorties which will be put aside when the King announces the boundaries of the Land.

Jerusalem is to be the capital of the world, the center of all religious and political activity. One of the most expressive statements regarding this was made by Zechariah:

> Yea, many peoples and strong nations shall come to seek the LORD of hosts in Jerusalem, and to pray before the LORD. Thus saith the LORD of hosts: In those days it shall come to pass that ten men shall take hold out of all languages of the nations, even shall take hold of the skirt of him that is a Jew, saying, We will go with you; for we have heard that God is with you (Zech. 8:22-23).

They will join in homage to God at the magnificent Temple described by Ezekiel chapters 40 through 44, where memorial worship to the sacrificial ministry of the Messiah will be observed.

The sheer splendor of this age, as described by the prophets, is thoroughly captivating. It will be marked by peace, equity, productivity, and righteousness. Isaiah summed it all up in these classic words taken from his description of the quality and extent of the kingdom: "They shall not hurt nor destroy in all my holy mountain; for the earth shall be full of the knowledge of the LORD, as the waters cover the sea" (Isa. 11:9).

Of course, central to everything is the King himself. All processes will flow about His supreme presence. God, in the person of the Messiah, will dwell in the midst of His people. There is little that can be said by way of explanation which can add an iota to the weight of this momentous revelation. Let Zechariah say it for us: "And the LORD shall be king over all the earth...And it shall come to pass that every one that is left of all the nations which came against Jerusalem shall even go up from year to year to worship the King, the LORD of hosts, and to keep the feast of tabernacles" (Zech. 14:9, 16).

A parting observation can constructively be offered. All that we have considered, which will take place during the Millennial Age of the Messiah's reign, is but a transcending prelude to the eternal glories God has prepared for His people.

Notes and References

THE LONG, LONELY ROAD

1 *Israel Pocket Library*, "Anti-Semitism" (Jerusalem: Keter Publishing House Jerusalem Ltd., 1974), pp. 105-106.
2 *Ibid.*, p.124.
3 *Ibid.*, p.111.
4 Philip Schaff, *History of the Christian Church*, V (Grand Rapids: William B. Eerdmans Co., 1970), pp. 240-241.

THEN THERE ARE CHRISTIANS

1 *Israel Pocket Library*, "Anti-Semitism" (Jerusalem: Keter Publishing House Jerusalem Ltd., 1974) p. 11.
2 *Ibid.*
3 *Ibid.*, p. 23.
4 Meir Kahane, "Christians for Zion," *The Jewish Press*, 24 January, 1975, p. 34.
5 Raphael Patai, Editor, *Encyclopedia of Zionism and Israel* (New York: Herzl Press/McGraw Hill, 1971).
6 Michael Comay, *Zionism and Israel — Questions and Answers* (Jerusalem: Keter Publishing House Jerusalem Ltd., 1976), p. 17.

BACK FROM THE DEAD

1 *Facts about Israel 1972* (Jerusalem: Keter Publishing House Jerusalem Ltd., 1974), p. 26.
2 Raphael Posner, General Editor, *Popular Judaica Library, The Return to Zion* (Jerusalem: Keter Publishing House Jerusalem Ltd., 1974), p. 26.
3 *Ibid.*
4 *Ibid.*, p. 24.
5 *Israel Pocket Library*, "History From 1880" (Jerusalem: Keter Publishing House Ltd., 1973), p. 43.

6 *Facts About Israel 1973* (Jerusalem: Division of Information, Ministry of Foreign Affairs, 1973), p. 34.

7 Ben Moshe, Editor, *David Ben Gurion* (Jerusalem: Youval Tal Ltd.), p. 44.

8 Posner, *Popular Judaica Library, The Return to Zion*, p. 114.

9 *Israel Pocket Library*, "History From 1880" (Jerusalem: Keter Publishing House Jerusalem Ltd., 1973), p. 141.

ON EAGLES' WINGS

1 Mark Twain, *The Innocents Abroad* (New York: 1966), p. 401.

2 Mark Twain, *Recollections of the East*, Vol. I, (London: 1845), p. 308.

3 *Facts About Israel 1972* (Jerusalem: Keter Publishing House Jerusalem Ltd., 1973), p. 116.

4 *Israel Pocket Library*, "Economy" (Keter Publishing House Jerusalem Ltd., 1973), p. 228.

WE ARE AT THE WALL

1 Larry Collins and Dominique Lapierre, *O Jerusalem* (New York: Simon and Schuster, 1973), p. 191.

2 Randolph S. and Winston S. Churchill, *The Six-Day War* (London: Heinemann, 1967), p. 191.

3 Teddy Kollek and Moshe Pearlman, *Jerusalem Sacred City of Mankind* (Jerusalem, Tel Aviv: Steinmatzky's Agency Ltd., 1975), p. 268.

A QUIET DAY IN OCTOBER

1 *Kippur* (Tel Aviv: Special Edition Publishers, 1973), p. 27.

2 *Ibid.*, p. 267.

3 Major-General Chaim Herzog, *The War of Atonement October 1973* (Boston, Toronto: Little Brown and Co., 1975), p. 278.

4 *Kippur* p. 113.

5 *Ibid.,* p. 115.

6 Herzog, *The War of Atonement October 1973*, p. 159.

7 *Kippur,* p. 8.

8 *The Yom Kippur War* (New York: Doubleday and Company Inc.), p. 134.

9 Herzog, *The War of Atonement October 1973*. p. 64.

10 *Kippur,* p. 181.

11 Herzog, *The War of Atonement October 1973*, p. 113.

12 *Ibid.,* p. 284.

THE STALKING BEAR

1 *Kippur* (Tel Aviv: Special Edition Publishers, 1973), p. 122.

2 *The Yom Kippur War* (New York: Doubleday and Company Inc.), p. 407.

3 *Russia Imperial Power in the Middle East* (Jerusalem: Carta Press, 1971), p. 28.

Bibliography

Churchill, Randolph S. and Winston S. *The Six-Day War*. London: Heinemann, 1967.

Collins, Larry and Lapierre, Dominique. *O Jerusalem*. New York: Simon and Schuster, 1973.

Edersheim, Alfred. *History of the Jewish Nation*. Grand Rapids: Baker Book House.

Herzog, Chaim. *The War of Atonement October 1973*. Boston, Toronto: Little Brown and Co., 1975.

Insight Team of the London Times. *The Yom Kippur War*. New York: Doubleday and Co.

Israel Pocket Library. *Anti-Semitism*. Jerusalem: Keter Publishing House Jerusalem Ltd., 1974.

———. *History Until 1880*. Jerusalem: Keter Publishing House Jerusalem Ltd., 1974.

———. *History From 1880*. Jerusalem: Keter Publishing House Jerusalem Ltd. 1974.

———. *Holocaust*. Jerusalem: Keter Publishing House Jerusalem Ltd., 1974.

Katz, Samuel. *Battleground; Fact and Fantasy in Palestine*. New York: Bantam Books, 1973.

Kollek, Teddy and Pearlman, Moshe. *Jerusalem Sacred City of Mankind*. Jerusalem: Steinmatzky's Agency Ltd., 1975.

Lorch, Netanel. *The Edge of the Sword; Israel's War of Independence*. Jerusalem: Masada Press Ltd., 1961.

———. *One Long War; Arab Versus Jew Since 1920*. New York: Herzl Press, 1976.

Rubinstein, Aryeh, Editor. *The Return to Zion*. Jerusalem: Keter Books, 1974

Schaff, Philip. *History of the Christian Church*, vol. V. Grand Rapids: William B. Eerdmans Co., 1970.